MODERN PHILOSOPHY

PHILOSOPHY

FROM 1500 CE TO THE PRESENT

The History of Philosophy

MODERN PHILOSOPHY

FROM 1500 CE TO THE PRESENT

EDITED BY BRIAN DUIGNAN, SENIOR EDITOR,
PHILOSOPHY AND RELIGION

Britannica®
Educational Publishing

IN ASSOCIATION WITH

ROSEN
EDUCATIONAL SERVICES

Published in 2011 by Britannica Educational Publishing
(a trademark of Encyclopædia Britannica, Inc.)
in association with Rosen Educational Services, LLC
29 East 21st Street, New York, NY 10010.

First Edition

Britannica Educational Publishing
Michael I. Levy: Executive Editor
J.E. Luebering: Senior Manager
Marilyn L. Barton: Senior Coordinator, Production Control
Steven Bosco: Director, Editorial Technologies
Lisa S. Braucher: Senior Producer and Data Editor
Yvette Charboneau: Senior Copy Editor
Kathy Nakamura: Manager, Media Acquisition
Brian Duignan: Senior Editor, Philosophy and Religion

Rosen Educational Services
Heather M. Moore Niver: Rosen Editor
Nelson Sá: Art Director
Cindy Reiman: Photography Manager
Matthew Cauli: Designer, Cover Design
Introduction by Brian Duignan

Library of Congress Cataloging-in-Publication Data

Modern philosophy : from 1500 CE to the present / edited by Brian Duignan.—1st ed.
    p. cm. -- (The history of philosophy)
"In association with Britannica Educational Publishing, Rosen Educational Services."
Includes bibliographical references and index.
ISBN 978-1-61530-145-4 (library binding)
1. Philosophy, Modern. I. Duignan, Brian.
B791.M655 2011
190—dc22

                                                                    2010011553

Manufactured in the United States of America

On the cover: Preeminent Western philosophers such as Friedrich Nietzsche enriched
modern philosophy, making it more pertinent than ever. *Hulton Archive/Getty Images*

On page 18: Sir Isaac Newton was the paramount figure of the scientific revolution of the
17th century. *Photos.com*

CONTENTS

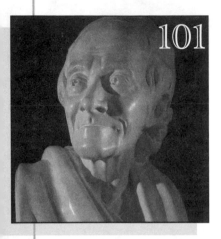

INTRODUCTION

RENATI·DES CARTES

PRINCIPIORUM
PHILOSOPHIÆ

Pars I, & II,

More Geometrico demonstratæ

PER

BENEDICTUM de SPINOZA *Amstelodamensem.*

Accesserunt Ejusdem

COGITATA METAPHYSICA,

In quibus difficiliores , quæ tam in parte Metaphysices generali , quàm speciali occurrunt , quæstiones breviter explicantur.

AMSTELODAMI,

Apud JOHANNEM RIEWERTS, *in vico vulgò dicto*, de Dirk van Assen-steeg, *sub signo Martyrologii.* 1663.

RENATI DES CARTES PRINCIPIORUM PHILOSOPHIÆ.
1re édition 1663 (Page de titre).

During the 14th century, European society suffered an unprecedented series of natural and human-made disasters, including famine, the Black Death, and numerous devastating and expensive wars. By the end of the century, the continent was a great deal poorer and much less populous than it had been in 1300. According to some historians, these calamities were the death knell of the Middle Ages: the drastic changes they brought about hastened the disappearance of characteristically medieval forms of political authority and social organization. More important, they also served to undermine confidence among late-medieval thinkers in dogmatic Christian and Aristotelian doctrines concerning the principles of the natural world, the proper structure and governance of human society, and the capacities and moral worth of human beings.

Other scholars see the 14th century as merely a temporary interruption in processes of social and intellectual transformation that had begun several centuries earlier and would have continued as they did whether or not the disasters of the period had ever occurred. However this may be, it is clear that by the late-15th century European society and intellectual culture had changed in significant ways. The national monarchies had completely eclipsed the power of the German "Holy Roman Empire," whose leader had been crowned by the pope since the early Middle Ages as the supreme secular authority on earth. In Italy, independent city-states such as Florence, Venice, and Milan were economically and militarily powerful, and

In 1664 René Descartes published Principles of Philosophy, *a compilation of his physics and metaphysics.* Time & Life Pictures/Getty Images

9

elsewhere the growth of commerce and manufacturing further increased the importance of cities and the merchant classes at the expense of the landed nobility.

This period was also marked by the rise of humanism, an intellectual movement that emphasized the dignity of the human individual. The humanists were responsible for the rediscovery and translation of a wealth of ancient Greek and Roman literary and philosophical texts, including the complete dialogues of Plato. They revered the "ancients," as they called the Greeks and Romans, for their intellectual rigour and integrity and for the freedom with which they pursued philosophical and scientific problems. In the latter respect ancient philosophers, in the estimation of the humanists, were far superior to the academic philosophers of previous centuries, the "Schoolmen" or Scholastics," who had been bound in their investigations to support, or at least not to contradict, the theology of the Roman Catholic Church. Indeed, the humanists regarded the Middle Ages (a term they invented) as a long period during which significant philosophical and literary activity had simply ceased. They understood themselves as the inheritors and standardbearers of Classical ideals against stultifying medieval orthodoxies. The term *Renaissance* was the somewhat judgmental invention of humanist sympathizers of the 19th century; nevertheless, it aptly conveys the intellectual renewal and reawakening that the humanists brought about.

Thus the humanists self-consciously took up where the ancients had left off. In philosophy, this is apparent not only in the new influence of ancient philosophical doctrines such as atomism and Stoicism but also in the revival of whole areas of philosophy that had been well developed in ancient times but relatively neglected during the Middle Ages—particularly political philosophy, epistemology (the study of knowledge), and ethics.

Modern Western philosophy conventionally begins in about 1500 and continues to the present day. This span of more than 500 years comprises four or five smaller periods: the Renaissance (1500–1600), the early modern period (1600–1700), the modern period (1700–1900)—sometimes subdivided into the Enlightenment (1700–1800) and the 19th century—and the contemporary period (1900–present).

Starting in the Renaissance, and especially in the 17th and early 18th centuries, political philosophy was developed in sophisticated ways—and from a purely secular perspective—to address the responsibilities of rulers and the justification of political authority in the new nation-states. The first major figure in this field was the Florentine statesman Niccòlo Machiavelli (1469–1527). He is often called the first political scientist because his analysis of statecraft and governance was realistic rather than idealistic. It took for granted the ways in which states (in his case, the city-states of Italy) and humans actually behave and prescribed on that basis certain guidelines that rulers should follow to acquire or maintain political power. Not since Aristotle had a philosopher considered states as they really are rather than as they ought to be. Not surprisingly, Machiavelli's frank advice, set forth in *Il Principe* (*The Prince*) and other works, was regarded by most readers as an endorsement of immorality and evil in the political sphere. The philosophical and empirical value of his work remained unrecognized for centuries.

Subsequent political philosophy in the early modern period was concerned with justifying the state and setting limits (however few) to the legitimate powers of the monarch or other ruler. In England, Thomas Hobbes (1588–1679) proposed a hypothetical "state of nature," assumed to precede the establishment of any political authority, in which the necessity of survival compelled each individual to be in constant violent conflict with every other. Human life was thus "solitary, poor, nasty, brutish, and short." To safeguard their lives, individuals entered into a "social contract" in which each agreed to surrender his natural right to govern himself to a sovereign authority on the condition that every other did the same. The sovereign, what Hobbes called the "Leviathan," would ensure peace and order by punishing those who committed violent acts. In essence, then, the absolute power of actual sovereigns is justified because without it human society would descend into an anarchic state of nature, a "war of all against all."

Later social-contract theorists, most importantly John Locke (1632–1704) in England and Jean-Jacques Rousseau (1712–78) in France, also saw the state as resulting from an agreement among individuals — or, in Rousseau's version, small groups of individuals — in a state of nature. For Locke, individuals are subject to a natural law of equality and have natural rights to life, liberty, and property; the contract creates a state with the power to protect these rights. More important, for Locke this function is the sole justification of the state's existence. It follows that citizens have a right of revolution against any state that fails to protect their rights. This view is the essence of the doctrine of political liberalism, which is embodied in the American Declaration of Independence (1776) as well as the French Declaration of the Rights of Man and of the Citizen (1789). Rousseau differed from Hobbes and Locke in holding that in the state of nature people were happy. With the gradual development of private property came inequality, envy, and strife. The state was accordingly created, by an essentially false social contract, by groups of rich individuals to protect their property and privileges against the poor. A true social contract, according to

Rousseau, would ensure the liberty and equality of all by enforcing the "general will" of all moral individuals.

After nearly two centuries, during which political philosophy was dominated by utilitarianism, the American political philosopher John Rawls employed the notion of a social contract as the basis of a new form of political liberalism. According to Rawls, fundamental political rights and freedoms, as well as minimal levels of social and economic equality, are guaranteed by political principles that people would agree to from behind a "veil of ignorance," where by hypothesis they do not know what positions in society they will occupy.

The modern development of epistemology was motivated by the rediscovery during the Renaissance of the historical works of Sextus Empiricus (flourished 3rd century CE), which summarized the Skeptical doctrines of the Hellenistic philosopher Pyrrhon of Elis (360–272 BCE) and his followers. The effort to solve the intractable problems of ancient Skepticism became one of the dominant themes of European philosophy. Eventually, two broad approaches developed, one influenced by Aristotle's emphasis on empirical observation and Sir Francis Bacon's (1561–1626) conception of human knowledge as founded upon the proper application of scientific method; the other by the mathematical metaphysics of Pythagoras and Plato and the spectacular successes of mathematical physics in the 16th and 17th centuries. According to empiricists, all (or nearly all) human knowledge is *a posteriori*, or derived from experience; according to rationalists, at least some human knowledge is *a priori*, or obtainable independently of experience. The task of epistemology, therefore, is to justify knowledge claims either by showing how their elements (e.g., concepts) are connected to something real in the outside world (empiricism) or by showing how knowledge claims are ultimately inferable from a set of basic propositions that are innate or otherwise knowable by the mind alone (rationalism). The most influential form of rationalism was that of René Descartes (1596–1650), who proposed to reconstruct the entire edifice of human knowledge on the foundation of the a priori proposition that for as long as he thinks, he must exist. (This proposition is often misleadingly interpreted as an inference: "I think, therefore I am." Strictly speaking, the radical skeptical position from which Descartes began would not have allowed him to be certain that this inference was carried out correctly.) The first well-developed empiricist theory of knowledge was that of Locke. Unfortunately, the basic empiricist assumption that all knowledge derives from experience, combined with gradually more rigorous analyses of what experience consists in, led to more consistent but also more extreme forms of empiricism in the philosophies of George Berkeley (1685–1753) and David Hume (1711–76). Hume, in fact, concluded that knowledge of a real connection between cause and effect is impossible and that therefore all scientific theories are rationally unfounded. Except for a brief period in the late 19th century, empiricism remained the dominant position in British and, later, American philosophy through the end of the 20th century. After a period of some 300 years, rationalism enjoyed a revival in the mid-20th century in the wake of scientific research on the innate mental structures that allow young children to learn new languages quickly and without apparent effort.

The gulf between rationalism and empiricism was bridged by the philosophy of Immanuel Kant (1724–1804). Kant argued that the common mistake of the two schools lay in the way the problem of knowledge was conceived: the problem was not how the mind conforms itself to objects but rather how objects conform themselves to the mind. A priori knowledge of broad features of the empirical world (such as the existence of causal relations) is possible because such features are part of the structure of the mind itself. Kant's philosophy became the foundation of later German idealism, in which the mind, self, or "Spirit" encompassed many more features of reality than Kant would have allowed, gradually blurring and eventually erasing the distinction between subject and object, knower and known. Kant's epistemology, recast in logical and linguistic terms, enjoyed a revival in the mid-20th century and remains an influential position in present-day discussions.

Although some philosophers of the Middle Ages made notable contributions to ethics, the field did not recover its ancient range and vitality until the rediscovery of Stoic and Epicurean texts during the Renaissance. Stoicism, which conceived of virtue and the human good in intellectual terms and emphasized a cultivated indifference to the travails of ordinary life, profoundly influenced the ethical views of many Renaissance and early modern philosophers, including Benedict de Spinoza (1632–77). The utilitarian ethics of Epicurus, who held that the only good is pleasure and the only evil pain, became the basis of utilitarianism, a major theoretical position in normative ethics since the 17th century. In the late 18th century, the philosopher and social reformer Jeremy Bentham articulated a utilitarian ethics that was noteworthy for its great consistency and rigour; it was developed and refined by his student and friend John Stuart Mill (1806–73) and later by Henry Sidgwick (1838–1900).

In the 18th century, a normative-ethical school later known as deontology opposed broadly utilitarian theories of conduct. According to deontology, the rightness or wrongness of an action depends solely on whether or not it conforms to a given moral rule—its actual or likely consequences are irrelevant. The supreme exponent of deontological ethics was Kant, who held that an action is right only if it is universalizable (i.e., only if one can will without contradiction that it become a universal law, or a law that is followed by everyone). The field of normative ethics was dominated by utilitarian and deontological theories until the mid-20th century, when the ethical philosophy of Aristotle became the basis of a school known as virtue ethics. At about the same time, the interest of philosophers in real-world issues such as war and peace, abortion, and the human treatment of animals spurred the growth of the new field of applied ethics. Work in applied ethics inspired social activism, entered discussions and debates on public policy, and in general made ethical philosophy influential in practical affairs to an extent not seen since the American and French revolutions.

In the pages of this book, the reader will be introduced to the greatest minds of modern Western philosophy. Their enormous contributions have made philosophy as it exists today richer, more historically informed, and more practically relevant than it has been in any period of its history.

EMPLEN. Sc.

CHAPTER 1

PHILOSOPHY IN THE RENAISSANCE

The philosophy of a period arises as a response to social need, and the development of philosophy in the history of Western civilization since the Renaissance has, thus, reflected the process in which creative philosophers have responded to the unique challenges of each stage in the development of Western culture itself.

The career of philosophy—how it views its tasks and functions, how it defines itself, the special methods it invents for the achievement of philosophical knowledge, the literary forms it adopts and uses, its conception of the scope of its subject matter, and its changing criteria of meaning and truth—hinges on the mode of its successive responses to the challenges of the social structure within which it arises. Thus, Western philosophy in the Middle Ages was primarily a Christian philosophy, complementing the divine revelation, reflecting the feudal order in its cosmology, and devoting itself in no small measure to the institutional tasks of the Roman Catholic Church. It was no accident that the major philosophical achievements of the 13th and 14th centuries were the work of churchmen who also happened to be professors of theology at the Universities of Oxford and Paris.

The Renaissance of the late 15th and 16th centuries presented a different set of problems and therefore

The University of Oxford proved to be fertile ground for significant philosophical achievements. Hulton Archive/Getty Images

suggested different lines of philosophical endeavour. What is called the European Renaissance followed the introduction of three novel mechanical inventions from the East: gunpowder, block printing from movable type, and the compass. The first was used to explode the massive fortifications of the feudal order and thus became an agent of the new spirit of nationalism that threatened the rule of churchmen—and, indeed, the universalist emphasis of the church itself—with a competing secular power. The second, printing, widely propagated knowledge, secularized learning, reduced the intellectual monopoly of an ecclesiastical elite, and restored the literary and philosophical classics of Greece and Rome. The third, the compass, increased the safety and scope of navigation, produced the voyages of discovery that opened up the Western Hemisphere, and symbolized a new spirit of physical adventure and a new scientific interest in the structure of the natural world.

Each invention, with its wider cultural consequences, presented new intellectual problems and novel philosophical tasks within a changing political and social environment. As the power of a single religious authority slowly eroded under the influence of the Protestant Reformation and as the prestige of the universal Latin language gave way to vernacular tongues, philosophers became less and less identified with their positions in the ecclesiastical hierarchy and more and more identified with their national origins. The works of Albertus Magnus (c. 1200–80), Thomas Aquinas (c. 1224–74), Bonaventure (c. 1217–74), and John Duns Scotus (1266–1308) were basically unrelated to the countries of their birth. The philosophy of Niccolò Machiavelli (1469–1527) was directly related to Italian experience, however, and that of Francis Bacon (1561–1626) was English to the core, as was that of Thomas Hobbes (1588–1679) in the early modern period. Likewise, the thought of René Descartes (1596–1650) set the standard and tone of intellectual life in France for 200 years.

Knowledge in the contemporary world is conventionally divided among the natural sciences, the social sciences, and the humanities. In the Renaissance, however, fields of learning had not yet become so sharply departmentalized. In fact, each division arose in the comprehensive and broadly inclusive area of philosophy. As the Renaissance mounted its revolt against the reign of religion and therefore reacted against the church, against authority, against Scholasticism, and against Aristotle (384–322 BCE), there was a sudden blossoming of interest in problems centring on humankind, civil society, and nature. These three areas corresponded exactly to the three dominant strands of Renaissance philosophy: humanism, political philosophy, and the philosophy of nature.

THE HUMANISTIC BACKGROUND

The term Middle Ages was coined by scholars in the 15th century to designate the interval between the downfall of the Classical world of Greece and Rome and its rediscovery at the beginning of their own century, a revival in which they felt they were participating. Indeed, the notion of a long period of cultural darkness had been expressed by Petrarch (1304–74) even earlier. Events during the last three centuries of the Middle Ages, particularly beginning in the 12th century, set in motion a series of social, political, and intellectual transformations that culminated in the Renaissance. These included the increasing failure of the Roman Catholic Church and the Holy Roman Empire to provide a stable and unifying framework for the organization of spiritual and material life, the rise in importance of city-states and national monarchies, the development of national languages, and the breakup of the old feudal structures.

Although the spirit of the Renaissance ultimately took many forms, it was expressed earliest by the intellectual movement called humanism. Humanism was initiated by secular men of letters rather than by the scholar-clerics who had dominated medieval intellectual life and had developed the Scholastic philosophy. Humanism began and achieved fruition first in Italy. Its predecessors were men like Dante (1265–1321) and Petrarch, and its chief protagonists included Gianozzo Manetti (1396–1459), Leonardo Bruni (c. 1370–1444), Marsilio Ficino (1433–99), Giovanni Pico della Mirandola (1463–94), Lorenzo Valla (1407–57), and Coluccio Salutati (1331–1406). The fall of Constantinople in 1453 provided humanism with a major boost, for many eastern scholars fled to Italy, bringing with them important books and manuscripts and a tradition of Greek scholarship.

Humanism had several significant features. First, it took human nature in all of its various manifestations and achievements as its subject. Second, it stressed the unity and compatibility of the truth found in all philosophical and theological schools and systems, a doctrine known as syncretism. Third, it emphasized the dignity of human beings. In place of the medieval ideal of a life of penance as the highest and noblest form of human activity, the humanists looked to the struggle of creation and the attempt to exert mastery over nature. Finally, humanism looked forward to a rebirth of a lost human spirit and wisdom. In the course of striving to recover it, however, the humanists assisted in the consolidation of a new spiritual and intellectual outlook and in the development of a new body of knowledge. The effect of humanism was to help people break free from the mental strictures imposed by religious orthodoxy, to inspire free inquiry and criticism,

Much to his chagrin, the work of Desiderius Erasmus helped spark the Reformation. Kean Collection/Hulton Archive/Getty Images

and to inspire a new confidence in the possibilities of human thought and creations.

From Italy the new humanist spirit and the Renaissance it engendered spread north to all parts of Europe, aided by the invention of printing, which allowed the explosive growth of literacy and the greater availability of Classical texts. Foremost among northern humanists was Desiderius Erasmus (1469–1536), whose *Praise of Folly* (1509) epitomized the moral essence of humanism in its insistence on heartfelt goodness as opposed to formalistic piety. The intellectual stimulation provided by humanists helped spark the Reformation, from which, however, many humanists, including Erasmus, recoiled. By the end of the 16th century, the battle of Reformation and Counter-Reformation had commanded much of Europe's energy and attention, while the intellectual life was poised on the brink of the Enlightenment.

THE IDEAL OF HUMANITAS

The history of the term *humanism* is complex but enlightening. It was first employed (as *humanismus*) by 19th-century German scholars to designate the Renaissance emphasis on classical studies in education. These studies were pursued and endorsed by educators known, as early as the late 15th century, as *umanisti*—that is, professors or students of Classical literature. The word *umanisti* derives from the *studia humanitatis*, a course of classical studies that, in the early 15th century, consisted of grammar, poetry, rhetoric, history, and moral philosophy. The *studia humanitatis* were held to be the equivalent of the Greek *paideia*. Their name was itself based on the Latin *humanitas*, an educational and political ideal that was the intellectual basis of the entire movement. Renaissance humanism in all its forms defined itself in its straining toward this ideal. No discussion of humanism, therefore, can have validity without an understanding of *humanitas*.

Humanitas meant the development of human virtue, in all its forms, to its fullest extent. The term thus implied not only such qualities as are associated with the modern word *humanity*—understanding, benevolence, compassion, mercy—but also more aggressive characteristics such as fortitude, judgment, prudence, eloquence, and even love of honour. Consequently, the possessor of *humanitas* could not be merely a sedentary and isolated philosopher or man of letters but was of necessity a participant in active life. Just as action without insight was held to be aimless and barbaric, insight without action was rejected as barren and imperfect. *Humanitas* called for a fine balance of action and contemplation, a balance born not of compromise but of complementarity. The goal of such fulfilled and balanced virtue was political, in the broadest sense of the word. The purview of Renaissance humanism included not only the education of the young but also the guidance of adults (including rulers) via philosophical poetry and strategic rhetoric. It included not only realistic social criticism but also utopian hypotheses, not only painstaking reassessments of history but also bold reshapings of the future. In short, humanism called for the comprehensive reform of culture, the transfiguration of what humanists termed the passive and ignorant society of the "dark" ages into a new order that would reflect and encourage the grandest human potentialities. Humanism had an evangelical dimension: it sought to project *humanitas* from the individual into the state at large.

The wellspring of *humanitas* was Classical literature. Greek and Roman thought, available in a flood of rediscovered or newly translated manuscripts, provided humanism with much of its basic structure and method. For Renaissance humanists, there was nothing dated or outworn about the writings of Plato (c. 428–348 BCE), Cicero (106–43 BCE), or Livy (59/64 BCE–17 CE). Compared with the typical productions of medieval Christianity, these pagan works had a fresh, radical, almost avant-garde tonality. Indeed, recovering the classics was to humanism tantamount to recovering reality. Classical philosophy, rhetoric, and history were seen as models of proper method—efforts to come to terms, systematically and without preconceptions of any kind, with perceived experience. Moreover, Classical thought considered ethics qua ethics, politics qua politics: it lacked the inhibiting dualism occasioned in medieval thought by the often-conflicting demands of secularism and Christian spirituality. Classical virtue, in examples of which the literature abounded, was not an abstract essence but a quality that could be tested in the forum or on the battlefield. Finally, Classical literature was rich in eloquence. In particular (because humanists were normally better at Latin than they were at Greek), Cicero was considered to be the pattern of refined and copious discourse. In eloquence humanists found far more than an exclusively aesthetic quality. As an effective means of moving leaders or fellow citizens toward one political course or another, eloquence was akin to pure power. Humanists cultivated rhetoric, consequently, as the medium through which all other virtues could be communicated and fulfilled.

Humanism, then, may be accurately defined as that Renaissance movement that had as its central focus the ideal of *humanitas*. The narrower definition of the Italian term *umanisti* notwithstanding, all the Renaissance writers who cultivated humanitas, and all their direct "descendants," may be correctly termed humanists.

Basic Principles and Attitudes

Underlying the early expressions of humanism were principles and attitudes that gave the movement a unique character and would shape its future development.

Classicism

Early humanists returned to the classics less with nostalgia or awe than with a sense of deep familiarity, an impression of having been brought newly into contact with expressions of an intrinsic and permanent human reality. Petrarch dramatized his feeling of intimacy with the classics by writing "letters" to Cicero and Livy. Salutati remarked with pleasure that possession of a copy of Cicero's letters would make it possible for him to talk with Cicero. Machiavelli would later immortalize this experience in a letter that described his own reading habits in ritualistic terms:

> *Evenings I return home and enter my study; and at its entrance I take off my everyday clothes, full of mud and dust, and don royal and courtly garments; decorously reattired, I enter into the ancient sessions of ancient men. Received amicably by them, I partake of such food as is mine only and for which I was born. There, without shame, I speak with them and ask them about the reason for their actions; and they in their humanity respond to me.*

Machiavelli's term *umanità* ("humanity"), meaning more than simply kindness, is a direct translation of the Latin *humanitas*. In addition to implying that he shared with the ancients a sovereign wisdom of human affairs, Machiavelli also describes that theory of reading as an active, and even aggressive, pursuit common among humanists. Possessing a text and understanding its words were insufficient. Analytic ability and a questioning attitude were essential before a reader could truly enter the councils of the great. These councils, moreover, were not merely serious and ennobling. They held secrets available only to the astute, secrets the knowledge of which could transform life from a chaotic miscellany into a crucially heroic experience. Classical thought offered insight into the heart of things. In addition, the classics suggested methods by which, once known, human reality could be transformed from an accident of history into an artifact of will. Antiquity was rich in examples—actual or poetic—of epic action, victorious eloquence, and applied understanding. Carefully studied and well employed, Classical rhetoric could implement enlightened policy, while Classical poetics could carry enlightenment into the very souls of human beings. In a manner that might seem paradoxical to more modern minds, humanists associated Classicism with the future.

REALISM

Early humanists shared in large part a realism that rejected traditional assumptions and aimed instead at the objective analysis of perceived experience. To humanism is owed the rise of modern social science, which emerged not as an academic discipline but rather as a practical instrument of social self-inquiry. Humanists avidly read history, taught it to their young, and, perhaps most important, wrote it themselves. They were confident that proper historical method, by extending across time their grasp of human reality, would enhance their active role in the present. For Machiavelli, who avowed to present people as they were and not as they ought to be, history would become the basis of a new political science. Similarly, direct experience took precedence over traditional wisdom. Francesco Guicciardini (1483–1540) later echoed the dictum of Leon Battista Alberti (1404–72), that an essential form of wisdom could be found only "at the public marketplace, in the theatre, and in people's homes":

I, for my part, know no greater pleasure than listening to an old man of uncommon prudence speaking of public and political matters that he has not learnt from books of philosophers but from experience and action; for the latter are the only genuine methods of learning anything.

Renaissance realism also involved the unblinking examination of human uncertainty, folly, and immorality. Petrarch's honest investigation of his own doubts and mixed motives is born of the same impulse that led Giovanni Boccaccio (1313–75) to conduct in the *Decameron* (1348–53) an encyclopaedic survey of human vices and disorders. Similarly critical treatments of society from a humanistic perspective would be produced later by Erasmus, Thomas More (1478–1535), Baldassare Castiglione (1478–1529), François Rabelais (*c.* 1494–1553), and Michel de Montaigne (1533–92). But it was typical of humanism that this moral criticism did not, conversely, postulate an ideal of absolute purity. Humanists asserted the dignity of normal earthly activities and even endorsed the pursuit of fame and the acquisition of wealth. The emphasis on a mature and healthy balance between mind and body, first implicit in Boccaccio, is evident in the work of Giannozzo Manetti, Francesco Filelfo (1398–1481), and Paracelsus (1493–1541) and eloquently embodied in Montaigne's final essay, "Of Experience." Humanistic tradition, rather than revolutionary inspiration, eventually led Francis Bacon to assert that the passions should become objects of systematic investigation. The realism of the humanists was, finally, brought to bear on the Roman Catholic Church, which they called into question not as a theological structure but as a political institution. Here as elsewhere, however, the intention was neither radical nor destructive. Humanism did not aim to remake humanity but rather aimed to reform social order through an understanding of what was basically and inalienably human.

CRITICAL SCRUTINY AND CONCERN WITH DETAIL

Humanistic realism bespoke a comprehensively critical attitude. Indeed, the productions of early humanism constituted a manifesto of independence, at least in the secular world, from all preconceptions and all inherited programs. The same critical self-reliance shown by Salutati in his textual emendations and Boccaccio in his interpretations of myth was evident in almost the whole range of humanistic endeavour. It was cognate with a new specificity, a profound concern with the precise details of perceived phenomena, that took hold across the arts and the literary and historical disciplines and would have profound effects on the rise of modern science. The increasing prominence of mathematics as an artistic principle and academic discipline was a testament to this development.

THE EMERGENCE OF THE INDIVIDUAL AND THE IDEA OF THE DIGNITY OF HUMANITY

These attitudes took shape in concord with a sense of personal autonomy that first was evident in Petrarch and later came to characterize humanism as a whole. An intelligence capable of critical scrutiny and self-inquiry was by definition a free intelligence. The intellectual virtue that could analyze experience was an integral part of that more extensive virtue that could, according to many humanists, go far in conquering fortune. The emergence of Renaissance individualism was not without its darker aspects. Petrarch and Alberti were alert to the sense of estrangement that accompanies intellectual and moral autonomy, while Machiavelli would depict, in *Il Principe* (1513; *The Prince*), a grim world in which the individual must exploit the weakness of the crowd or fall victim to its indignities. But happy or sad, the experience of the individual had taken on a heroic tone. Parallel with individualism arose, as a favourite humanistic theme, the idea of human dignity. Backed by medieval sources but more sweeping and insistent in their approach, spokesmen such as Petrarch, Manetti, Valla, and Ficino asserted humans' earthly preeminence and unique potentialities. In his noted *De hominis dignitate oratio* (1486; *Oration on the Dignity of Man*), Pico della Mirandola conveyed this notion with unprecedented vigour. Pico asserted that humanity had been assigned no fixed character or limit by God but instead was free to seek its own level and create its own future. No dignity, not even divinity itself, was forbidden to human aspiration. Pico's radical affirmation of human capacity shows the influence of Ficino's contemporary translations of the Hermetic writings—the purported works of the Egyptian god Hermes Trismegistos. Together with the even bolder 16th-century formulations of this position by Paracelsus and Giordano Bruno (1548–1600), the *Oratio* betrays a rejection of the early humanists' emphasis on balance and moderation. Rather, it suggests the straining toward absolutes that would characterize major elements of later humanism.

ACTIVE VIRTUE

The emphasis on virtuous action as the goal of learning was a founding principle of humanism and (although sometimes sharply challenged) continued to exert a strong influence throughout the course of the movement. Salutati, the learned chancellor of Florence whose words could batter cities, represented in word and deed the humanistic ideal of an armed wisdom, that combination of philosophical understanding and powerful rhetoric that alone could effect virtuous policy and reconcile the rival claims of action and contemplation. In *De ingenuis moribus et liberalibus studiis* (1402–03; "On the Manners of a Gentleman and Liberal Studies"), a treatise that influenced Guarino Veronese (1374–1460) and Vittorino da Feltre (1378–1446), Pietro Paolo Vergerio (*c.* 1369–1444) maintained that just and beneficent action was the purpose of humanistic education. His words were echoed by Alberti in *Della famiglia* (1435–44; "On the Family"):

> *As I have said, happiness cannot be gained without good works and just and righteous deeds.... The best works are those that benefit many people. Those are most virtuous, perhaps, that cannot be pursued without strength and nobility. We must give ourselves to manly effort, then, and follow the noblest pursuits.*

Matteo Palmieri (1406–75) wrote that

> *the true merit of virtue lies in effective action, and effective action is impossible without the faculties that are necessary for it. He who has nothing to give cannot be generous. And he who loves solitude can be neither just, nor strong, nor experienced in those things that are of importance in government and in the affairs of the majority.*

Palmieri's philosophical poem, *La città di vita* (1465; "The City of Life"), developed the idea that the world was divinely ordained to test human virtue in action. Later humanism would broaden and diversify the theme of active virtue. Machiavelli saw action not only as the goal of virtue but also (via historical understanding of great deeds of the past) as the basis for wisdom. Castiglione, in his highly influential *Il cortegiano* (1528; *The Courtier*), developed in his ideal courtier a psychological model for active virtue, stressing moral awareness as a key element in just action. Rabelais used the idea of active virtue as the basis for anticlerical satire. In his profusely humanistic *Gargantua* (1534), he has the active hero Friar John save a monastery from enemy attack while the monks sit uselessly in the church choir, chanting meaningless Latin syllables. John later asserts that had he been present, he would have used his manly strength to save Jesus from crucifixion, and he castigates the Apostles for betraying Christ "after a good meal." Endorsements of active virtue, as will be shown, would also characterize the work of English humanists from Sir Thomas Elyot (*c.* 1490–1546) to John Milton (1608–74). They typify the sense of social responsibility—the instinctive association of learning with politics and morality—that stood at the heart of the movement. As Salutati put it, "One must stand in the line of battle, engage in close combat, struggle for justice, for truth, for honour."

HUMANIST THEMES IN RENAISSANCE THOUGHT

Although the humanists were not primarily philosophers and belonged to no single school of formal thought, they had a great deal of influence on philosophy. They searched out and copied the works of ancient authors, developed critical tools for establishing accurate texts from variant manuscripts, made translations from Latin and Greek, and wrote commentaries that reflected their broad learning as well as their new standards and points of view. Aristotle's authority remained preeminent, especially in logic and physics, but humanists were instrumental in the revival of other Greek scientists and other ancient philosophies, including Stoicism, Skepticism, and various forms of

Platonism (such as the eclectic Neoplatonist and gnostic doctrines of the Alexandrian schools known as Hermetic philosophy). All of these were to have far-reaching effects on the subsequent development of European thought. While humanists had a variety of intellectual and scholarly aims, it is fair to say that, like the ancient Romans, they preferred moral philosophy to metaphysics. Their faith in the moral benefits of poetry and rhetoric inspired generations of scholars and educators. Their emphasis on eloquence, worldly achievement, and fame brought them readers and patrons among merchants and princes and employment in government chancelleries and embassies.

Humanists were secularists in the sense that language, literature, politics, and history, rather than "sacred subjects," were their central interests. They defended themselves against charges from conservatives that their preference for classical authors was ruining Christian morals and faith, arguing that a solid grounding in the classics was the best preparation for the Christian life. This was already a perennial debate, almost as old as Christianity itself, with neither side able to sway the other. There seems to have been little atheism or dechristianization among the humanists or their pupils, but there were efforts to redefine the relationship between religious and secular culture. Petrarch struggled with the problem in his book *Secretum meum* (1342–43, revised 1353–58), in which he imagines himself chastized by St. Augustine of Hippo (354–430) for his pursuit of worldly fame. Even the most celebrated of Renaissance themes, the dignity of humanity, best known in Pico della Mirandola's *Oration*, was derived in part from the Church Fathers. Created in the image and likeness of God, people were free to shape their destiny, but human destiny was defined within a Christian, Neoplatonic context of contemplative thought.

*You will have the power to sink to the lower forms of life,
which are brutish. You will have the power, through your own
judgment, to be reborn into the higher forms, which are divine.*

Perhaps because Italian politics were so intense and
innovative, the tension between traditional Christian
teachings and actual behaviour was more frankly acknowledged in political thought than in most other fields. The
leading spokesman of the new approach to politics was
Machiavelli. Best known as the author of *The Prince,* a
short treatise on how to acquire power, create a state, and
keep it, Machiavelli dared to argue that success in politics
had its own rules. This so shocked his readers that they
coined his name into synonyms for the Devil ("Old Nick")
and for crafty, unscrupulous tactics (Machiavellian). No
other name, except perhaps that of the Borgias, so readily
evokes the image of the wicked Renaissance, and, indeed,
Cesare Borgia (*c.* 1475–1507) was one of Machiavelli's chief
models for *The Prince.*

Machiavelli began with the not unchristian axiom that
people are immoderate in their ambitions and desires and
likely to oppress each other whenever free to do so. To get
them to limit their selfishness and act for the common
good should be the lofty, almost holy, purpose of governments. How to establish and maintain governments that
do this was the central problem of politics, made acute for
Machiavelli by the twin disasters of his time, the decline of
free government in the city-states and the overrunning
of Italy by French, German, and Spanish armies. In *The
Prince* he advocated his emergency solution: Italy needed a
new leader, who would unify the people, drive out "the barbarians," and reestablish civic virtue. In the more detached
and extended discussion of *Discorsi sopra la prima deca di Tito
Livio* (1517; *Discourses on the First Ten Books of Livy*), however,
he analyzed the foundations and practice of republican

government, still trying to explain how stubborn and defective human material was transformed into political community.

Machiavelli was influenced by humanist culture in many ways, including his reverence for classical antiquity, concern with politics, and effort to evaluate the impact of fortune as against free choice in human life. The "new path" in politics that he announced in *The Prince* was an effort to provide a guide for political action based on the lessons of history and his own experience as a foreign secretary in Florence. In his passionate republicanism he showed himself to be the heir of the great humanists of a century earlier who had expounded the ideals of free citizenship and explored the uses of classicism for the public life.

At the beginning of the 15th century, when the Visconti rulers of Milan were threatening to overrun Florence, Salutati had rallied the Florentines by reminding them that their city was "the daughter of Rome" and the legatee of Roman justice and liberty. Salutati's pupil, Leonardo Bruni, who also served as chancellor, took up this line in his panegyrics of Florence and in his *Historiarum Florentini populi libri XII* ("Twelve Books of Histories of the Florentine People"). Even before the rise of Rome, according to Bruni, the Etruscans had founded free cities in Tuscany, so the roots of Florentine liberty went very deep. There equality was recognized in justice and opportunity for all citizens, and the claims of individual excellence were rewarded in public offices and public honours. This close relation between freedom and achievement, argued Bruni, explained Florence's superiority in culture as well as in politics. Florence was the home of Italy's greatest poets, the pioneer in both vernacular and Latin literature, and the seat of the Greek revival and of eloquence. In short, Florence was the centre of the *studia humanitatis*.

As political rhetoric, Bruni's version of Florentine superiority was magnificent and no doubt effective. It inspired the Florentines to hold out against Milanese aggression and to reshape their identity as the seat of "the rebirth of letters" and the champions of freedom. But as a theory of political culture, this "civic humanism" represented the ideal rather than the reality of 15th-century communal history. Even in Florence, where after 1434 the Medici family held a grip on the city's republican government, opportunities for the active life began to fade. The emphasis in thought began to shift from civic humanism to Neoplatonist idealism and to the kind of utopian mysticism represented by Pico della Mirandola's *Oration*. At the end of the century, Florentines briefly put themselves into the hands of the millennialist Dominican preacher Girolamo Savonarola (1452–98), who envisioned the city as the "New Jerusalem" rather than as a reincarnation of ancient Rome. Still, even Savonarola borrowed from the civic tradition of the humanists for his political reforms (and for his idea of Florentine superiority) and in so doing created a bridge between the republican past and the crisis years of the early 16th century.

Machiavelli got his first job in the Florentine chancellery in 1498, the year of Savonarola's fall from power. Dismissing the friar as one of history's "unarmed prophets" who are bound to fail, Machiavelli was convinced that the precepts of Christianity had helped make the Italian states sluggish and weak. He regarded religion as an indispensable component of human life, but statecraft as a discipline based on its own rules and no more to be subordinated to Christianity than were jurisprudence or medicine. The simplest example of the difference between Christian and political morality is provided by warfare, where the use of deception, so detestable in every other kind of action, is necessary, praiseworthy, even glorious. In the *Discourses,* Machiavelli commented upon a Roman defeat:

> *This is worth noting by every citizen who is called upon to give counsel to his country, for when the very safety of the country is at stake there should be no question of justice or injustice, of mercy or cruelty, of honour or disgrace, but putting every other consideration aside, that course should be followed which will save her life and liberty.*

Machiavelli's own country was Florence. When he wrote that he loved his country more than he loved his soul, he was consciously forsaking Christian ethics for the morality of civic virtue. His friend and countryman Francesco Guicciardini shared his political morality and concern for politics but lacked his faith that a knowledge of ancient political wisdom would redeem the liberty of Italy. Guicciardini was an upper-class Florentine who chose a career in public administration and devoted his leisure to writing history and reflecting on politics. He was steeped in the humanist traditions of Florence and was a dedicated republican, notwithstanding the fact—or perhaps because of it—that he spent his entire career in the service of the Medici and rose to high positions under them. But Guicciardini, more skeptical and aristocratic than Machiavelli, was also half a generation younger, and he was schooled in an age that was already witnessing the decline of Italian autonomy.

In 1527 Florence revolted against the Medici a second time and established a republic. As a confidant of the Medici, Guicciardini was passed over for public office and retired to his estate. One of the fruits of this enforced leisure was the so-called *Cose fiorentine* (*Florentine Affairs*), an

Francesco Guicciardini doubted that people could learn from the past and shape the course of events. Private Collection/Alinari/The Bridgeman Art Library

unfinished manuscript on Florentine history. Although it generally follows the classic form of humanist civic history, the fragment contains some significant departures from this tradition. No longer is the history of the city treated in isolation. Guicciardini was becoming aware that the political fortunes of Florence were interwoven with those of Italy as a whole and that the French invasion of Italy in 1494 was a turning point in Italian history. He returned to public life with the restoration of the Medici in 1530 and was involved in the events leading to the tightening of the imperial grip upon Italy, the humbling of the papacy, and the final transformation of the republic of Florence into a hereditary Medici dukedom. Frustrated in his efforts to influence the rulers of Florence, he again retired to his villa to write. But instead of taking up the unfinished manuscript on Florentine history, he chose a subject commensurate with his changed perspective on Italian affairs. The result was his *Storia d'Italia* (*History of Italy*). Although still in the humanist form and style, it was in substance a fulfillment of the new tendencies already evident in the earlier work: criticism of sources, great attention to detail, avoidance of moral generalizations, and shrewd analysis of character and motive.

The *History of Italy* has rightly been called a tragedy, for it demonstrates how, out of stupidity and weakness, people make mistakes that gradually narrow the range of their freedom to choose alternative courses and thus influence events until, finally, they are trapped in the web of fortune. This view of history was already far from the world of Machiavelli, not to mention that of the civic humanists. Where Machiavelli believed that *virtù* — bold and intelligent initiative — could shape, if not totally control, *fortuna* — the play of external forces — Guicciardini was skeptical about people's ability to learn from the past and pessimistic about the individual's power to shape the course of events. All that was left, he believed, was to understand. Guicciardini wrote his histories of Florence and of Italy to show what people were like and explain how they had reached their present circumstances. Human dignity, then, consisted not in the exercise of will to shape destiny but in the use of reason to contemplate and perhaps to tolerate fate. In taking a new, hard look at the human condition, Guicciardini represents the decline of humanist optimism.

Northern Humanism

The resumption of urban growth in the second half of the 15th century coincided with the diffusion of Renaissance ideas and educational values. Humanism offered linguistic and rhetorical skills that were becoming indispensable for nobles and commoners seeking careers in diplomacy and government administration, while the Renaissance ideal of the perfect gentleman was a cultural style that had great appeal in this age of growing courtly refinement. At first many who wanted a humanist education went to Italy, and many foreign names appear on the rosters of the Italian universities. By the end of the century, however, such northern cities as London, Paris, Antwerp, and Augsburg were becoming centres of humanist activity rivaling Italy's. The development of printing, by making books cheaper and more plentiful, also quickened the diffusion of humanism.

A textbook convention, heavily armoured against truth by constant reiteration, states that northern humanism (i.e., humanism outside Italy) was essentially Christian in spirit and purpose, in contrast to the essentially secular nature of Italian humanism. In fact, however, the program of Christian humanism had been laid out by Italian humanists of the stamp of Lorenzo Valla, one of the founders of classical philology, who showed how the critical methods used to study the classics ought to be applied to problems of biblical exegesis and translation as well as church history. That this program only began to be carried out in the 16th century, particularly in the countries of northern Europe (and Spain), is a matter of chronology rather than of geography. In the 15th century, the necessary skills, particularly the knowledge of Greek, were possessed by a few scholars. A century later, Greek was a regular part of the humanist curriculum, and Hebrew was becoming much better known, particularly after Johannes Reuchlin (1455–1522) published his Hebrew grammar in 1506. Here, too, printing was a crucial factor, for it made available a host of lexicographical and grammatical handbooks and allowed the establishment of normative biblical texts and the comparison of different versions of the Bible.

Christian humanism was more than a program of scholarship, however; it was fundamentally a conception of the Christian life that was grounded in the rhetorical, historical, and ethical orientation of humanism itself. That it came to the fore in the early 16th century was the result of a variety of factors, including the spiritual stresses of rapid social change and the inability of the ecclesiastical establishment to cope with the religious needs of an increasingly literate and self-confident laity. By restoring the gospel to the centre of Christian piety, the humanists believed they were better serving the needs of ordinary people. They attacked Scholastic theology as an arid intellectualization of simple faith and deplored the tendency of religion to become a ritual practiced vicariously through a priest. Humanists also despised the whole late-medieval apparatus of relic mongering, hagiology, indulgences, and image worship and ridiculed it in their writings, sometimes with devastating effect. According to the Christian humanists, the fundamental law of Christianity was the law of love as revealed by Jesus Christ in the Gospel. Love, peace, and simplicity should be the aims of the good Christian, and the life of Christ his perfect model.

The chief spokesman for this point of view was Desiderius Erasmus, the most influential humanist of his day. Erasmus and his colleagues were uninterested in dogmatic differences and were early champions of religious toleration. In this they were out of tune with the changing times. The outbreak of the Reformation polarized European society along confessional lines, with the paradoxical result that the Christian humanists, who had done so much to lay the groundwork for religious reform, ended by being suspect on both sides—by the Roman Catholics as subversives who (as it was said of Erasmus) had "laid the egg that [Martin] Luther hatched" and by the Protestants as hypocrites who had abandoned the cause of reformation out of cowardice or ambition. Toleration belonged to the future, after the killing in the name of Christ sickened and passions had cooled.

HUMANISM AND PHILOSOPHY

Renaissance humanism was predicated upon the victory of rhetoric over dialectic and of Plato over Aristotle as the cramped format of Scholastic philosophical method gave way to a Platonic discursiveness. Much of this transformation had been prepared by Italian scholarly initiative in the early 15th century. Lorenzo Valla used the recently discovered manuscript of *Institutio oratoria* by Quintilian (35–c. 96) to create new forms of rhetoric and textual criticism. But even more important was the rebirth of an enthusiasm for the philosophy of Plato in Medici Florence and at the cultivated court of Urbino. Precisely to service this enthusiasm, Marsilio Ficino, head of the Platonic

Academy, translated the entire Platonic corpus into Latin by the end of the 15th century.

Except in the writings of Pico della Mirandola and Giordano Bruno, the direct influence of Platonism on Renaissance metaphysics is difficult to trace. The Platonic account of the moral virtues, however, was admirably adapted to the requirements of Renaissance education, serving as a philosophical foundation of the Renaissance ideal of the courtier and gentleman. Yet Plato also represented the importance of mathematics and the Pythagorean attempt to discover the secrets of the heavens, the earth, and the world of nature in terms of number and exact calculation. This aspect of Platonism influenced Renaissance science as well as philosophy. The scientists Nicolaus Copernicus (1473–1543), Johannes Kepler (1571–1630), and Galileo Galilei (1564–1642) owe a great deal to the general climate of Pythagorean confidence in the explanatory power of number.

Platonism also affected the literary forms in which Renaissance philosophy was written. Although the earliest medieval Platonists, such as Augustine and John Scotus Erigena (810–c. 877), occasionally used the dialogue form, later Scholastics abandoned it in favour of the formal treatise, of which the great "summae" of Alexander of Hales (c. 1170–1245) and Thomas Aquinas were pristine examples. The Renaissance rediscovery of the Platonic dialogues suggested the literary charm of this conversational method to humanists, scientists, and political philosophers alike. Bruno put forth his central insights in a dialogue, *De la causa, principio e uno* (1584; *Concerning the Cause, Principle, and One*); Galileo presented his novel mechanics in his *Dialogo sopra i due massimi sistemi del mondo, tolemaico e copernicano* (1632; *Dialogue Concerning the Two Chief World Systems—Ptolemaic and Copernican*); and even Machiavelli's

Dell'arte della guerra (1521; *The Art of War*) takes the form of a genteel conversation in a quiet Florentine garden.

The recovery of the Greek and Latin classics, which was the work of humanism, profoundly affected the entire field of Renaissance and early modern philosophy and science through the ancient schools of philosophy to which it once more directed attention. In addition to Platonism, the most notable of these schools were atomism, Skepticism, and Stoicism. *De rerum natura*, by the Epicurean philosopher Lucretius (flourished 1st century BCE), influenced Galileo, Bruno, and later Pierre Gassendi (1592–1655), a modern follower of Epicurus (341–270 BCE), through the insights into nature reflected in this work. The recovery of *Outlines of Pyrrhonism*, by Sextus Empiricus (flourished 3rd century CE), reprinted in 1562, produced a skeptical crisis in French philosophy that dominated the period from Montaigne to Descartes. And the Stoicism of Seneca (4 BCE–65 CE) and Epictetus (55–*c.* 135) became almost the official ethics of the Renaissance, figuring prominently in the *Essays* (1580–88) of Montaigne, in the letters that Descartes wrote to Princess Elizabeth of Bohemia (1618–79) and to Queen Christina of Sweden (1626–89), and in the later sections of the *Ethics* (1675) of the Dutch-Jewish philosopher Benedict de Spinoza (1632–77).

POLITICAL PHILOSOPHY

As secular authority replaced ecclesiastical authority and the dominant interest of the age shifted from religion to politics, it was natural that the rivalries of the national states and their persistent crises of internal order should raise with renewed urgency philosophical problems, practically dormant since pre-Christian times, about the nature and the moral status of political power. This new preoccupation with national unity, internal security, state power, and international justice stimulated the growth of political philosophy in Italy, France, England, and Holland.

Machiavelli, sometime state secretary of the Florentine republic, explored techniques for the seizure and retention of power in ways that seemed to exalt "reasons of state" above morality. His *The Prince* and *Discourses on the First Ten Books of Livy* codified the actual practices of Renaissance diplomacy for the next 100 years. In fact, Machiavelli was motivated by patriotic hopes for the ultimate unification of Italy and by the conviction that the moral standards of contemporary Italians needed to be elevated by restoring the ancient Roman virtues. More than half a century later, the French political philosopher Jean Bodin (1530–96) insisted that the state must possess a single, unified, and absolute power. He thus developed in detail the doctrine of national sovereignty as the source of all legal legitimacy.

In England, Thomas Hobbes, who was to become tutor to the future king Charles II (1630–85), developed the fiction that in the "state of nature" that preceded civilization, "every man's hand [was] raised against every other" and human life was accordingly "solitary, poor, nasty, brutish, and short." A social contract was thus agreed upon to convey all private rights to a single sovereign in return for general protection and the institution of a reign of law. Because law is simply "the command of the sovereign," Hobbes at once turned justice into a by-product of power and denied any right of rebellion except when the sovereign becomes too weak to protect the commonwealth or to hold it together.

In Holland, a prosperous and tolerant commercial republic in the 17th century, the issues of political philosophy took a different form. The Dutch East India Company commissioned a great jurist, Hugo Grotius (1583–1645), to write a defense of their trading rights and their free access to the seas, and the resulting two treatises, *The Freedom of the Seas* (1609) and *On the Law of War and Peace* (1625), were the first significant codifications of international law. Their philosophical originality lay, however, in the fact that, in defending the rights of a small, militarily weak nation against the powerful states of England, France, and Spain, Grotius was led to a preliminary investigation of the sources and validity of the concept of natural law—the notion that inherent in human reason and immutable even against the willfulness of sovereign states are imperative considerations of natural justice and moral responsibility, which must serve as a check against the arbitrary exercise of vast political power.

In general, the political philosophy of the Renaissance and the early modern period was dualistic: it was haunted, even confused, by the conflict between political necessity and general moral responsibility. Machiavelli, Bodin, and Hobbes asserted claims that justified the actions of Italian despotism and the absolutism of the Bourbon and Stuart dynasties. Yet Machiavelli was obsessed with the problem of human virtue, Bodin insisted that even the sovereign ought to obey the law of nature (that is, to govern in accordance with the dictates of natural justice), and Hobbes found in natural law the rational motivation that causes a person to seek security and peace. In the end, Renaissance and early modern political philosophy advocated the doctrines of Thrasymachus, who held that right is what is in the interests of the strong, but it could never finally escape a twinge of Socratic conscience.

PHILOSOPHY OF NATURE

Philosophy in the modern world is a self-conscious discipline. It has managed to define itself narrowly, distinguishing itself on the one hand from religion and on the other from exact science. But this narrowing of focus came about quite late in its history—certainly not before the 18th century. The earliest philosophers of ancient Greece were theorists of the physical world. Pythagoras and Plato were at once philosophers and mathematicians, and in Aristotle there is no clear distinction between philosophy and natural science. The Renaissance and early modern period continued this breadth of conception characteristic of the Greeks. Galileo and Descartes were at once mathematicians, physicists, and philosophers, while physics retained the name *natural philosophy* at least until the death of Sir Isaac Newton (1642–1727).

Had the thinkers of the Renaissance been painstaking in the matter of definition (which they were not), they might have defined philosophy, on the basis of its actual practice, as "the rational, methodical, and systematic consideration of humankind, civil society, and the natural world." Philosophy's areas of interest would thus not have been in doubt, but the issue of what constitutes "rational, methodical, and systematic consideration" would have been extremely controversial. Because knowledge advances through the discovery and advocacy of new philosophical methods and because these diverse methods depend for their validity on prevailing philosophical criteria of truth, meaning, and importance, the crucial philosophical quarrels of the 16th and 17th centuries were at bottom quarrels about method. It is this issue, rather than any disagreement over subject matter or areas of interest, that divided the greatest Renaissance philosophers.

The great new fact that confronted the Renaissance was the immediacy, the immensity, and the uniformity of the natural world. But what was of primary importance was the new perspective through which this fact was

Self-portrait by Leonardo da Vinci, chalk drawing. 1512; in the Palazzo Reale, Turin, Italy. Alinari/Art Resource, New York

interpreted. To the Schoolmen of the Middle Ages, the universe was hierarchical, organic, and God-ordained. To the philosophers of the Renaissance, it was pluralistic, machinelike, and mathematically ordered. In the Middle Ages, scholars thought in terms of purposes, goals, and divine intentions. Renaissance scholars thought in terms of forces, mechanical agencies, and physical causes. All this was clarified by the end of the 15th century. Within the early pages of the *Notebooks* of Leonardo da Vinci (1452–1519), the great Florentine artist and polymath, occur the following three propositions:

1. Since experience has been the mistress of whoever has written well, I take her as my mistress, and to her on all points make my appeal.
2. Instrumental or mechanical science is the noblest and above all others the most useful, seeing that by means of it all animated bodies which have movement perform all their actions.
3. There is no certainty where one can neither apply any of the mathematical sciences, nor any of those which are based upon the mathematical sciences.

Here are enunciated respectively (1) the principle of empiricism, (2) the primacy of mechanistic science, and (3) faith in mathematical explanation. It is upon these three doctrines, as upon a rock, that Renaissance and early modern science and philosophy were built. From each of Leonardo's theses descended one of the great streams of Renaissance and early modern philosophy: from the empirical principle the work of Bacon, from mechanism the work of Hobbes, and from mathematical explanation the work of Descartes.

Any adequate philosophical treatment of scientific method recognizes that the explanations offered by science are both empirical and mathematical. In Leonardo's thinking, as in scientific procedure generally, although there need be no conflict between these two ideals, they do represent two opposite poles, each capable of excluding the other. The peculiar accidents of Renaissance scientific achievement did mistakenly suggest their incompatibility, for the revival of medical studies on the one hand and the blooming of mathematical physics on the other emphasized opposite virtues in scientific methodology. This polarity was represented by the figures of Andreas Vesalius (1514–64) and Galileo.

Vesalius, a Flemish physician, astounded all of Europe with the unbelievable precision of his anatomical dissections and drawings. Having invented new tools for this precise purpose, he successively laid bare the vascular, neural, and muscular systems of the human body. This procedure seemed to demonstrate the virtues of empirical method, of experimentation, and of inductive generalization on the basis of precise and disciplined observation.

Only slightly later, Galileo, following in the tradition already established by Copernicus and Kepler, attempted to do for terrestrial and sidereal movement what Vesalius had managed for the structure of the human body—creating his physical dynamics, however, on the basis of hypotheses derived from mathematics. In Galileo's work, all the most original scientific impulses of the Renaissance were united: the interest in Hellenistic mathematics, experimental use of new instruments such as the telescope, and underlying faith that the search for certainty in science is reasonable because the motions of all physical bodies are comprehensible in mathematical terms. Galileo's work also deals with some of the recurrent themes of 16th- and 17th-century philosophy: atomism (which describes the changes of gross physical bodies in terms of the motions of their parts), the reduction of qualitative differences to quantitative differences, and the resultant important distinction between "primary" and "secondary" qualities. The former qualities—including shape, extension, and specific gravity—were deemed part of nature and therefore real. The latter—such as colour, odour, taste, and relative position—were taken to be simply the effect of the motions of physical bodies on perceiving minds and therefore ephemeral, subjective, and essentially irrelevant to the nature of physical reality.

The remainder of this chapter discusses in detail the lives and work of the most important philosophers of the Renaissance.

GIOVANNI PICO DELLA MIRANDOLA

(b. Feb. 24, 1463, Mirandola, duchy of Ferrara [Italy]—d. Nov. 17, 1494, Florence [Italy])

Giovanni Pico della Mirandola was an Italian scholar and Platonist philosopher who was known for his syncretistic method of taking the best elements from other philosophies and combining them in his own work, as illustrated in his "Oration on the Dignity of Man."

His father, Giovanni Francesco Pico, prince of the small territory of Mirandola, provided for his precocious child's thorough humanistic education at home. Pico then studied canon law at Bologna and Aristotelian philosophy at Padua and visited Paris and Florence, where he learned Hebrew, Aramaic, and Arabic. At Florence he met the leading Platonist philosopher Marsilio Ficino.

Introduced to Kabbala (Jewish mysticism), Pico became the first Christian scholar to use Kabbalistic doctrine in support of Christian theology. In 1486, planning to defend

900 theses he had drawn from diverse Greek, Hebrew, Arabic, and Latin writers, he invited scholars from all of Europe to Rome for a public disputation. For the occasion he composed his celebrated *Oratio*. A papal commission, however, denounced 13 of the theses as heretical, and the assembly was prohibited by Pope Innocent VIII. Despite his ensuing *Apologia* for the theses, Pico thought it prudent to flee to France but was arrested there. After a brief imprisonment he settled in Florence, where he became associated with the Platonic Academy, under the protection of the Florentine prince Lorenzo de' Medici. Except for short trips to Ferrara, Pico spent the rest of his life there. He was absolved from the charge of heresy by Pope Alexander VI in 1492. Toward the end of his life, he came under the influence of the strictly orthodox Girolamo Savonarola, the enemy of Lorenzo and eventually a martyr.

Pico's unfinished treatise against enemies of the church includes a discussion of the deficiencies of astrology. Although this critique was religious rather than scientific in its foundation, it influenced the astronomer Johannes Kepler, whose studies of planetary movements underlie modern astronomy. Pico's other works include an exposition of Genesis under the title *Heptaplus* (Greek *hepta,* "seven"), indicating his seven points of argument, and a synoptic treatment of Plato and Aristotle, of which the completed work *De ente et uno* (*Of Being and Unity*) is a portion. Pico's works were first collected in *Commentationes Joannis Pici Mirandulae* (1495–96).

NICCOLÒ MACHIAVELLI

(b. May 3, 1469, Florence, Italy—d. June 21, 1527, Florence)

Niccolò Machiavelli was an Italian political philosopher, statesman, and secretary of the Florentine republic whose most famous work, *The Prince*, brought him a reputation as an atheist and an immoral cynic.

EARLY LIFE AND POLITICAL CAREER

From the 13th century onward, Machiavelli's family was wealthy and prominent, holding on occasion Florence's most important offices. His father, Bernardo, a doctor of laws, was nevertheless among the family's poorest members. Barred from public office in Florence as an insolvent debtor, Bernardo lived frugally, administering his small landed property near the city and supplementing his meagre income from it with earnings from the restricted and almost clandestine exercise of his profession.

Bernardo kept a library in which Niccolò must have read, but little is known of Niccolò's education and early life in Florence, at that time a thriving centre of philosophy and a brilliant showcase of the arts. He attended lectures by Marcello Virgilio Adriani, who chaired the Studio Fiorentino. He learned Latin well and probably knew some Greek, and he seems to have acquired the typical humanist education that was expected of officials of the Florentine Chancery.

In a letter to a friend in 1498, Machiavelli writes of listening to the sermons of Girolamo Savonarola, a Dominican friar who moved to Florence in 1482 and in the 1490s attracted a party of popular supporters with his thinly veiled accusations against the government, the clergy, and the pope. Although Savonarola, who effectively ruled Florence for several years after 1494, was featured in *The Prince* (1513) as an example of an "unarmed prophet" who must fail, Machiavelli was impressed with his learning and rhetorical skill. On May 24, 1498, Savonarola was hanged as a heretic and his body burned in the public square. Several days later, emerging from obscurity at the

Although Niccolò Machiavelli was branded as an atheist and an immoral cynic, the final chapter of The Prince *has led many to deem him a patriot.* Hulton Archive/Getty Images

age of 29, Machiavelli became head of the second chancery (*cancelleria*), a post that placed him in charge of the republic's foreign affairs in subject territories. How so young a man could be entrusted with so high an office remains a mystery, particularly because Machiavelli apparently never served an apprenticeship in the chancery. He held the post until 1512, having gained the confidence of Piero Soderini (1452–1522), the gonfalonier (chief magistrate) for life in Florence from 1502.

During his tenure at the second chancery, Machiavelli persuaded Soderini to reduce the city's reliance on mercenary forces by establishing a militia (1505), which Machiavelli subsequently organized. He also undertook diplomatic and military missions to the court of France; to Cesare Borgia, the son of Pope Alexander VI (reigned 1492–1503); to Pope Julius II (reigned 1503–13), Alexander's successor; to the court of Holy Roman Emperor Maximilian I (reigned 1493–1519); and to Pisa (1509 and 1511).

In 1503, one year after his missions to Cesare Borgia, Machiavelli wrote a short work, *Del modo di trattare i sudditi della Val di Chiana ribellati* (*On the Way to Deal with the Rebel Subjects of the Valdichiana*). Anticipating his later *Discourses on the First Ten Books of Livy*, a commentary on the ancient Roman historian, in this work he contrasts the errors of Florence with the wisdom of the Romans and declares that in dealing with rebellious peoples one must either benefit them or eliminate them. Machiavelli also was a witness to the bloody vengeance taken by Cesare on his mutinous captains at the town of Sinigaglia (Dec. 31, 1502), of which he wrote a famous account. In much of his early writings, Machiavelli argues that "one should not offend a prince and later put faith in him."

In 1503 Machiavelli was sent to Rome for the duration of the conclave that elected Pope Julius II, an enemy of the Borgias, whose election Cesare had unwisely aided.

Machiavelli watched Cesare's decline and, in a poem (the first *Decennali*), celebrated his imprisonment, a burden that "he deserved as a rebel against Christ." Altogether, Machiavelli embarked on more than 40 diplomatic missions during his 14 years at the chancery.

In 1512 the Florentine republic was overthrown and the gonfalonier deposed by a Spanish army that Julius II had enlisted into his Holy League. The Medici family returned to rule Florence, and Machiavelli, suspected of conspiracy, was imprisoned, tortured, and sent into exile in 1513 to his father's small property in San Casciano, just south of Florence. There he wrote his two major works, *The Prince* and *Discourses on Livy*, both of which were published after his death. He dedicated *The Prince* to Lorenzo di Piero de' Medici (1492–1519), ruler of Florence from 1513 and grandson of Lorenzo de' Medici (1449–92). When, on Lorenzo's death, Cardinal Giulio de' Medici (1478–1534) came to govern Florence, Machiavelli was presented to the cardinal by Lorenzo Strozzi (1488–1538), scion of one of Florence's wealthiest families, to whom he dedicated the dialogue *The Art of War*.

Machiavelli was first employed in 1520 by the cardinal to resolve a case of bankruptcy in Lucca, where he took the occasion to write a sketch of its government and to compose his *La vita di Castruccio Castracani da Lucca* (1520; *The Life of Castruccio Castracani of Lucca*). Later that year the cardinal agreed to have Machiavelli elected official historian of the republic, a post to which he was appointed in November 1520 with a salary of 57 gold florins a year, later increased to 100. In the meantime, he was commissioned by the Medici pope Leo X (reigned 1513–21) to write a discourse on the organization of the government of Florence. Machiavelli criticized both the Medici regime and the succeeding republic he had served and boldly advised the pope to restore the republic, replacing the unstable mixture of republic and principality then prevailing. Shortly thereafter, in May 1521, he was sent for two weeks to the Franciscan chapter at Carpi, where he improved his ability to "reason about silence." Machiavelli faced a dilemma about how to tell the truth about the rise of the Medici in Florence without offending his Medici patron.

After the death of Pope Leo X in 1521, Cardinal Giulio, Florence's sole master, was inclined to reform the city's government and sought out the advice of Machiavelli, who replied with the proposal he had made to Leo X. In 1523, following the death of Pope Adrian VI, the cardinal became Pope Clement VII, and Machiavelli worked with renewed enthusiasm on an official history of Florence. In June 1525 he presented his *Istorie Fiorentine* (*Florentine Histories*) to the pope, receiving in return a gift of 120 ducats. In April 1526, Machiavelli was made chancellor of the Procuratori delle Mura to superintend Florence's fortifications. At this time the pope had formed a Holy League at Cognac against Holy Roman Emperor Charles V (reigned 1519–56), and Machiavelli went with the army to join his friend Francesco Guicciardini (1482–1540), the pope's lieutenant, with whom he remained until the sack of Rome by the emperor's forces brought the war to an end in May 1527. Now that Florence had cast off the Medici, Machiavelli hoped to be restored to his old post at the chancery. But the few favours that the Medici had doled out to him caused the supporters of the free republic to look upon him with suspicion. Denied the post, he fell ill and died within a month.

WRITINGS

In office Machiavelli wrote a number of short political discourses and poems (the *Decennali*) on Florentine history. It was while he was out of office and in exile, however, that the "Florentine Secretary," as Machiavelli came to be called, wrote the works of political philosophy for which he is remembered. In his most noted letter (Dec. 10, 1513), he described one of his days: in the morning walking in the woods, in the afternoon drinking and gambling with friends at the inn, and in the evening reading and reflecting in his study, where, he says, "I feed on the food that alone is mine and that I was born for." In the same letter, Machiavelli remarks that he has just composed a little work on princes—a "whimsy"—and thus lightly introduces arguably the most famous book on politics ever written, the work that was to give the name Machiavellian to the teaching of worldly success through scheming deceit.

About the same time that Machiavelli wrote *The Prince* (1513, published in 1532), he was also writing a completely different book, *Discourses on Livy* (published in 1531). They are distinguished from his other works by the fact that in the dedicatory letter to each he says that it contains everything he knows. The dedication of the *Discourses on Livy* presents the work to two of Machiavelli's friends, who he says are not princes but deserve to be, and criticizes the sort of begging letter he appears to have written in dedicating *The Prince*. The two works differ also in substance and manner. *The Prince* is mostly concerned with princes—particularly new princes—and is short, easy to read, and, according to many, dangerously wicked, whereas the *Discourses on Livy* is a "reasoning" that is long, difficult, and full of advice on how to preserve republics. Every thoughtful treatment of Machiavelli has had to come to terms with the differences between his two most important works.

THE PRINCE

The first and most persistent view of Machiavelli is that of a teacher of evil. The German-born American philosopher

Leo Strauss (1899–1973) begins his interpretation from this point. *The Prince* is in the tradition of the "Mirror for Princes" (i.e., books of advice that enabled princes to see themselves as though reflected in a mirror), which began with the *Cyropaedia* by the Greek historian Xenophon (431–350 BCE) and continued into the Middle Ages. Prior to Machiavelli, works in this genre advised princes to adopt the best prince as their model, but Machiavelli's version recommends that a prince go to the "effectual truth" of things and forgo the standard of "what should be done" lest he bring about his ruin. To maintain himself, a prince must learn how not to be good and use or not use this knowledge "according to necessity." An observer would see such a prince as guided by necessity, and from this standpoint Machiavelli can be interpreted as the founder of modern political science, a discipline based on the actual state of the world as opposed to how the world might be in utopias such as Plato's *Republic* of Plato or Augustine's *City of God*. This second, amoral interpretation can be found in works by the German historian Friedrich Meinecke (1862–1954) and the German philosopher Ernst Cassirer (1874–1945). The amoral interpretation fastens on Machiavelli's frequent resort to "necessity" to excuse actions that might otherwise be condemned as immoral. Machiavelli also advises the use of prudence in particular circumstances, however; and although he sometimes offers rules or remedies for princes to adopt, he does not seek to establish exact or universal laws of politics in the manner of modern political science.

Machiavelli divides principalities into those that are acquired and those that are inherited. In general, he argues that the more difficult it is to acquire control over a state, the easier it is to hold on to it. The reason for this is that the fear of a new prince is stronger than the love for a hereditary prince; hence, the new prince, who relies on "a dread of punishment that never forsakes you," will succeed, but a prince who expects his subjects to keep their promises of support will be disappointed. The prince will find that "each wants to die for him when death is at a distance," but, when the prince needs his subjects, they generally decline to serve as promised. Thus, every prince, whether new or old, must look upon himself as a new prince and learn to rely on "one's own arms," both literally in raising one's own army and metaphorically in not relying on the goodwill of others.

The new prince relies on his own virtue, but if virtue is to enable him to acquire a state, it must have a new meaning distinct from the New Testament virtue of seeking peace. Machiavelli's notion of *virtù* requires the prince to be concerned foremost with the art of war and to seek not merely security but also glory, for glory is included in necessity. *Virtù* for Machiavelli is virtue not for its own sake but rather for the sake of the reputation it enables princes to acquire. For example, liberality does not aid a prince, because the recipients may not be grateful, and lavish displays necessitate taxing of the prince's subjects, who will despise him for it. Thus, a prince should not be concerned if he is considered stingy, because this vice enables him to rule. Similarly, a prince should not care about being deemed cruel as long as the cruelty is "well used." Machiavelli sometimes uses *virtù* in the traditional sense, too, as in a famous passage on Agathocles (361–289 BCE), the self-styled king of Sicily, whom Machiavelli describes as a "most excellent captain" but one who came to power by criminal means. Of Agathocles, Machiavelli writes that "one cannot call it virtue to kill one's citizens, betray one's friends, to be without faith, without mercy and without religion." Yet in the very next sentence he speaks of "the virtue of Agathocles," who did all these things. Virtue, according to Machiavelli, aims to reduce the power of fortune over human affairs because fortune keeps men from relying on themselves. At first Machiavelli admits that fortune rules half of men's lives, but then, in an infamous metaphor, he compares fortune to a woman who lets herself be won more by the impetuous and the young, "who command her with more audacity," than by those who proceed cautiously. Machiavelli cannot simply dismiss or replace the traditional notion of moral virtue, which gets its strength from the religious beliefs of ordinary people. His own virtue of mastery coexists with traditional moral virtue yet also makes use of it. A prince who possesses the virtue of mastery can command fortune and manage people to a degree never before thought possible.

In the last chapter of *The Prince*, Machiavelli writes a passionate "exhortation to seize Italy and to free her from the barbarians"—apparently France and Spain, which had been overrunning the disunited peninsula. He calls for a redeemer, mentioning the miracles that occurred as Moses led the Israelites to the promised land, and closes with a quotation from a patriotic poem by Petrarch (1304–74). The final chapter has led many to a third interpretation of Machiavelli as a patriot rather than as a disinterested scientist.

THE DISCOURSES ON LIVY

Like *The Prince*, the *Discourses on Livy* admits of various interpretations. One view, elaborated separately in works by the political theorists J.G.A. Pocock and Quentin Skinner in the 1970s, stresses the work's republicanism and locates Machiavelli in a republican tradition that starts with Aristotle and continues through the organization of the medieval city-states, the renewal of classical political philosophy in Renaissance humanism, and the establishment of the contemporary American republic. This interpretation focuses on Machiavelli's various pro-republican remarks, such as his statement that the multitude is wiser and more constant than a prince and his emphasis in the *Discourses on Livy* on the republican virtue of self-sacrifice as a way of combating corruption. Yet Machiavelli's republicanism does not rest on the usual republican premise that power is safer in the hands of many than it is in the hands of one. To the contrary, he asserts that to found or reform a republic, it is necessary to "be alone." Any ordering must depend on a single mind. Thus, Romulus "deserves excuse" for killing Remus, his brother and partner in the founding of Rome, because it was for the common good. This statement is as close as Machiavelli ever came to saying "the end justifies the means," a phrase closely associated with interpretations of *The Prince*.

Republics need the kind of leaders that Machiavelli describes in *The Prince*. These "princes in a republic" cannot govern in accordance with justice, because those who get what they deserve from them do not feel any obligation. Nor do those who are left alone feel grateful. Thus, a prince in a republic will have no "partisan friends" unless he learns "to kill the sons of Brutus," using violence to make examples of enemies of the republic and, not incidentally, of himself. To reform a corrupt state presupposes a good man, but to become a prince presupposes a bad man. Good men, Machiavelli claims, will almost never get power, and bad men will almost never use power for a good end. Yet, because republics become corrupt when the people lose the fear that compels them to obey, the people must be led back to their original virtue by sensational executions reminding them of punishment and reviving their fear. The apparent solution to the problem is to let bad men gain glory through actions that have a good outcome, if not a good motive.

In the *Discourses on Livy*, Machiavelli favours the deeds of the ancients above their philosophy, reproaching his contemporaries for consulting ancient jurists for political wisdom rather than looking to the actual history of Rome. He argues that the factional tumults of the Roman republic, which were condemned by many ancient writers, actually made Rome free and great. Moreover, although Machiavelli was a product of the Renaissance (and is often portrayed as its leading exponent) he also criticized it, particularly for the humanism it derived from Plato, Aristotle, and Cicero. He called for "new modes and orders" and compared himself to the explorers of unknown lands in his time. His emphasis on the effectual truth led him to seek the hidden springs of politics in fraud and conspiracy, examples of which he discussed with apparent relish. It is notable that, in both *The Prince* and the *Discourses on Livy*, the longest chapters are on conspiracy.

Throughout his two chief works, Machiavelli sees politics as defined by the difference between the ancients and the moderns: the ancients are strong, the moderns weak. The moderns are weak because they have been formed by Christianity, and, in three places in the *Discourses on Livy*, Machiavelli boldly and impudently criticizes the Roman Catholic church and Christianity itself. For Machiavelli the church is the cause of Italy's disunity; the clergy is dishonest and leads people to believe "that it is evil to say evil of evil"; and Christianity glorifies suffering and makes the world effeminate. But Machiavelli leaves it unclear whether he prefers atheism, paganism, or a reformed Christianity, writing later, in a letter dated April 16, 1527 (only two months before his death): "I love my country more than my soul."

JEAN BODIN

(b. 1530, Angers, France — d. June 1596, Laon, France)

Jean Bodin was a French political philosopher whose exposition of the principles of stable government was widely influential in Europe at a time when medieval systems were giving way to centralized states. He is widely credited with introducing the concept of sovereignty into legal and political thought.

In 1551 Bodin went to the University of Toulouse to study civil law. He remained there as a student and later as a teacher until 1561, when he abandoned the teaching of law for its practice and returned to Paris as *avocat du roi* ("king's advocate") just as the civil wars between Roman Catholics and Huguenots were beginning. In 1571 he entered the household of the king's brother, François, duc d'Alençon, as master of requests and councillor. He appeared only once on the public scene, as deputy of the third estate for Vermandois at the Estates-General of Blois in 1576. His uninterested conduct on that occasion lost him royal favour. He opposed the projected resumption of war on the Huguenots in favour of negotiation, and he also opposed the suggested alienation, or sale, of royal domains by the French king Henry III (reigned 1574–89) as damaging to the monarchy. When the duc d'Alençon died in 1583, Bodin retired to Laon as *procurateur* to the presidial court. He remained there until his death from the plague 13 years later.

Bodin's principal writing, *The Six Bookes of a Commonweale* (1576), won him immediate fame and was influential in western Europe into the 17th century. The bitter experience of civil war and its attendant anarchy in France had turned Bodin's attention to the problem of how to secure order and authority. Bodin thought that the secret lay in recognition of the sovereignty of the state and argued that the distinctive mark of the state is supreme power. This power is unique; absolute, in that no limits of time or competence can be placed upon it; and self-subsisting, in that it does not depend for its validity on the consent of the subject. Bodin assumed that governments command by divine right because government is instituted by providence for the well-being of humanity. Government consists essentially of the power to command, as expressed in the making of laws. In a well-ordered state, this power is exercised subject to the principles of divine and natural law. In other words, the Ten Commandments are enforced, and certain fundamental rights, chiefly liberty and property, are extended to those governed. But should these conditions be violated, the sovereign still commands and may not be resisted by his subjects, whose whole duty is obedience to their ruler. Bodin distinguished only three types of political systems—monarchy, aristocracy, and democracy—according to whether sovereign power rests in one person, in a minority, or in a majority. Bodin himself preferred a monarchy that was kept informed of the people's needs by a parliament or representative assembly.

GIORDANO BRUNO

(b. 1548, Nola, near Naples—d. Feb. 17, 1600, Rome)

Giordano Bruno was an Italian philosopher, astronomer, mathematician, and occultist whose theories anticipated modern science. The most notable of these were his theories of the infinite universe and the multiplicity of worlds, in which he rejected the traditional geocentric (or Earth-centred) astronomy and intuitively went beyond the Copernican heliocentric (Sun-centred) theory, which still maintained a finite universe with a sphere of fixed stars. Bruno is, perhaps, chiefly remembered for the tragic death he suffered at the stake because of the tenacity with which he maintained his unorthodox ideas at a time when both the Roman Catholic and the Reformed churches were reaffirming rigid Aristotelian and Scholastic principles in their struggle for the evangelization of Europe.

EARLY LIFE

Bruno was the son of a professional soldier. He was named Filippo at his baptism and was later called "il Nolano," after the place of his birth. In 1562 Bruno went to Naples to study the humanities, logic, and dialectics (argumentation). He was impressed by the lectures of G.V. de Colle, who was known for his tendencies toward Averroism (i.e., the thought of a number of Western Christian philosophers who drew their inspiration from the interpretation of Aristotle put forward by the Arabic philosopher Averroës) and by his own reading of works on memory devices and the arts of memory (mnemotechnical works).

In 1565 he entered the Dominican convent of San Domenico Maggiore in Naples and assumed the name Giordano, but his unorthodox attitudes spurred suspicions of heresy. Nevertheless, in 1572 he was ordained a priest. During the same year he was sent back to the Neapolitan convent to continue his study of theology. In July 1575 Bruno completed the prescribed course, which generated in him an annoyance at theological subtleties. After he read two forbidden commentaries by Erasmus and freely discussing the Arian heresy, which denied the divinity of Christ, a trial for heresy was prepared against him by the provincial father of the order. So he fled to Rome in February 1576. There he found himself unjustly accused of a murder. A second excommunication process was started, and in April 1576 he fled again. He abandoned the Dominican Order, and, after wandering in northern Italy, he went in 1578 to Geneva, where he earned his living by proofreading. Bruno formally embraced Calvinism. After publishing a broadsheet against a Calvinist professor, however, he discovered that the Reformed Church was no less intolerant than the Catholic. He was arrested, excommunicated, rehabilitated after retraction, and finally allowed to leave the city. He moved to France, first to Toulouse—where he unsuccessfully sought to be absolved by the Catholic Church but was nevertheless appointed to a lectureship in philosophy—and then in 1581 to Paris.

In Paris Bruno at last found a congenial place to work and teach. Despite the strife between the Catholics and the Huguenots (French Protestants), the court of Henry III was then dominated by the tolerant faction of the Politiques (moderate Catholics, sympathizers of the Protestant king of Navarre, Henry of Bourbon, who became the heir apparent to the throne of France in 1584). Bruno's religious attitude was compatible with this group, and he received the protection of the French king, who appointed him one of his temporary *lecteurs royaux*. In 1582 Bruno published three works in which he explored new means to attain an intimate knowledge of reality. He also published a vernacular comedy, *Il candelaio* (1582; "The Candlemaker"), which, through a vivid representation of contemporary Neapolitan society, constituted a protest against the moral and social corruption of the time.

In the spring of 1583 Bruno moved to London with an introductory letter from Henry III for his ambassador Michel de Castelnau. He was soon attracted to Oxford, where, during the summer, he started a series of lectures in which he expounded the Copernican theory maintaining the reality of the movement of the Earth. Because of the hostile reception of the Oxonians, however, he went back to London as the guest of the French ambassador. He frequented the court of Elizabeth I (reigned 1558–1603) and became associated with such influential figures as the statesman and poet Sir Philip Sidney (1554–86) and Robert Dudley (1532–88), the earl of Leicester.

WORKS

In February 1584, Bruno was invited to discuss his theory of the movement of the Earth with some Oxonian doctors, but the encounter degenerated into a quarrel. A few days later he started writing his Italian dialogues, which constitute the first systematic exposition of his philosophy. There are six dialogues, three cosmological—on the theory of the universe—and three moral. In the *Cena de le Ceneri* (1584; "The Ash Wednesday Supper"), he not only reaffirmed the reality of the heliocentric theory but also suggested that the universe is infinite, constituted of innumerable worlds substantially similar to those of the solar system. In the same dialogue he anticipated his fellow Italian astronomer Galileo Galilei by maintaining that the Bible should be followed for its moral teaching but not for its astronomical implications. He also strongly criticized the manners of English society and the pedantry of the Oxonian doctors. In the *De la causa, principio e uno* (1584; *Concerning the Cause, Principle, and One*) he elaborated the physical theory on which his conception of the universe was based: "form" and "matter" are intimately united and constitute the "one." Thus, the traditional dualism of the Aristotelian physics was reduced by him to a monistic conception of the world, implying the basic unity of all substances and the coincidence of opposites in the infinite unity of Being. In the *De l'infinito universo e mondi* (1584; *On the Infinite Universe and Worlds*), he developed his cosmological theory by systematically criticizing Aristotelian physics. He also formulated his Averroistic view of the relation between philosophy and religion, according to which religion is considered as a means to instruct and govern ignorant people, philosophy as the discipline of the elect who are able to behave themselves and govern others.

The *Spaccio de la bestia trionfante* (1584; *The Expulsion of the Triumphant Beast*), the first dialogue of his moral trilogy, is a satire on contemporary superstitions and vices, embodying a strong criticism of Christian ethics (particularly the Calvinistic principle of salvation by faith alone, to which Bruno opposes an exalted view of the dignity of all human activities). The *Cabala del cavallo Pegaseo* (1585; *Cabal of the Horse Pegasus*), similar to but more pessimistic than the previous work, includes a discussion of the relationship between the human soul and the universal soul, concluding with the negation of the absolute individuality of the former. In the *De gli eroici furori* (1585; *The Heroic Frenzies*), Bruno, making use of Neoplatonic imagery, treats the attainment of union with the infinite One by the human soul and exhorts humanity to the conquest of virtue and truth.

In October 1585 Bruno returned to Paris, where he found a changed political atmosphere. Henry III had abrogated the edict of pacification with the Protestants, and the King of Navarre had been excommunicated. Far from adopting a cautious line of behaviour, however, Bruno entered into a polemic with a protégé of the Catholic party, the mathematician Fabrizio Mordente, whom he ridiculed in four *Dialogi,* and in May 1586 he dared to attack Aristotle publicly in his *Centum et viginti articuli de natura et mundo adversus Peripateticos* ("120 Articles on Nature and the World Against the Peripatetics"). The Politiques disavowed him, and Bruno left Paris.

He went to Germany, where he wandered from one university city to another, lecturing and publishing a variety of minor works, including the *Articuli centum et sexaginta* (1588; "160 Articles") against contemporary mathematicians and philosophers, in which he expounded his conception of religion—a theory of the peaceful coexistence of all religions based upon mutual understanding and the freedom of reciprocal discussion. At Helmstedt, however, in January 1589 he was excommunicated by the local Lutheran Church. He remained in Helmstedt until the spring, completing works on natural and mathematical magic (posthumously published) and working on three Latin poems: *De triplici minimo et mensura* ("On the Threefold Minimum and Measure"), *De monade, numero et figura* ("On the Monad, Number, and Figure"), and *De immenso, innumerabilibus et infigurabilibus* ("On the Immeasurable and Innumerable"). The trio of poems reelaborate the theories expounded in the Italian dialogues and develop Bruno's concept of an atomic basis of matter and being. To publish these, he went in 1590 to Frankfurt am Main, where the senate rejected his application to stay. Nevertheless, he took up residence in the Carmelite convent, lecturing to Protestant doctors and acquiring a reputation of being a "universal man" who, the Prior thought, "did not possess a trace of religion" and who "was chiefly occupied in writing and in the vain and chimerical imagining of novelties."

FINAL YEARS

In August 1591, at the invitation of the Venetian patrician Giovanni Mocenigo, Bruno made the fatal move of returning to Italy. At the time such a move did not seem to be too much of a risk: Venice was by far the most liberal of the Italian states; the European tension had been temporarily eased after the death of the intransigent pope Sixtus V in 1590; the Protestant Henry of Bourbon was now on the throne of France, and a religious pacification seemed to be imminent. Furthermore, Bruno was still looking for an academic platform from which to expound his theories, and he must have known that the chair of mathematics at the University of Padua was then vacant. Indeed, he went almost immediately to Padua and, during the late summer of 1591, started a private course of lectures for German students and composed the *Praelectiones geometricae* ("Lectures on Geometry") and *Ars deformationum* ("Art of Deformation"). At the beginning of the winter, when it appeared that he was not going to receive the chair (it was offered to Galileo in 1592), he returned to Venice, as the guest of Mocenigo, and took part in the discussions of progressive Venetian aristocrats who, like Bruno, favoured philosophical investigation irrespective of its theological implications.

Bruno's liberty came to an end when Mocenigo, disappointed by his private lessons from Bruno on the art of memory and resentful of Bruno's intention to go back to Frankfurt to have a new work published, denounced him to the Venetian Inquisition in May 1592 for his heretical theories. Bruno was arrested and tried. He defended himself by admitting minor theological errors, emphasizing, however, the philosophical rather than the theological character of his basic tenets. Just as the Venetian stage of the trial seemed to be proceeding in a way that was favourable to Bruno, the Roman Inquisition demanded his extradition. On Jan. 27, 1593, Bruno entered the jail of the Roman palace of the Sant'Uffizio (Holy Office).

During the seven-year Roman period of the trial, Bruno at first developed his previous defensive line, disclaiming any particular interest in theological matters and reaffirming the philosophical character of his speculation.

This distinction did not satisfy the inquisitors, who demanded an unconditional retraction of his theories. Bruno then made a desperate attempt to demonstrate that his views were compatible with the Christian conception of God and creation. The inquisitors rejected his arguments and pressed him for a formal retraction. Bruno finally declared that he had nothing to retract and that he did not even know what he was expected to retract. At that point, Pope Clement VIII ordered that he be sentenced as an impenitent and pertinacious heretic. On Feb. 8, 1600, when the death sentence was formally read to him, he addressed his judges, saying, "Perhaps your fear in passing judgment on me is greater than mine in receiving it." Not long after, he was brought to the Campo de' Fiori, his tongue in a gag, and burned alive.

CHAPTER 2

EARLY MODERN PHILOSOPHY

The scientific contrast between Vesalius's rigorous observational techniques and Galileo's reliance on mathematics was similar to the philosophical contrast between the experimental method of Francis Bacon (1561–1626) and the emphasis on a priori reasoning (reasoning independently of experience) of René Descartes (1596–1650). Indeed, these differences can be conceived in more abstract terms as the contrast between empiricism (the view that human knowledge ultimately originates in or is justified by experience) and rationalism (the view that human knowledge ultimately originates in or is justified by reason). This theme dominated the philosophical controversies of the 17th and 18th centuries and was hardly resolved before the advent of the German Enlightenment philosopher Immanuel Kant (1724–1804). The earliest empiricist philosophers of the modern period were Bacon and the English materialist Thomas Hobbes (1588–1679). The great rationalist philosophers were Descartes, the Dutch-Jewish thinker Benedict de Spinoza (1632–77), and the German polymath Gottfried Wilhelm Leibniz (1646–1714).

THE EMPIRICISM OF FRANCIS BACON

Sir Francis Bacon was the outstanding apostle of early modern empiricism. Less an original metaphysician or cosmologist than the advocate of a vast new program for the advancement of learning and the reformation of scientific method, Bacon conceived of philosophy as a new technique of reasoning that would reestablish natural science on a firm foundation. In the *Advancement of Learning* (1605), he charted the map of knowledge: history, which depends on the human faculty of memory; poetry, which depends on imagination; and philosophy, which depends on reason. To reason, however, Bacon assigned a completely experiential function. Fifteen years later, in his *Novum Organum*, he made this clear. Because, he said, "we have as yet no natural philosophy which is pure, . . . the true business of philosophy must be . . . to apply the understanding . . . to a fresh examination of particulars." A technique for "the fresh examination of particulars" thus constituted his chief contribution to philosophy.

Bacon's empiricism was not raw or unsophisticated. His concept of fact and his belief in the primacy of observation led him to formulate laws and generalizations. His enduring place in the history of philosophy lies, however, in his single-minded advocacy of experience as the only source of valid knowledge and in his profound enthusiasm for the perfection of natural science. It is in this sense that "the Baconian spirit" was a source of inspiration for generations of later philosophers and scientists.

BACON'S SCHEME

Bacon drew up an ambitious plan for a comprehensive work that was to appear under the title of *Instauratio Magna* ("The Great Instauration"), but like many of his literary schemes, it was never completed. Its first part, *De Augmentis Scientiarum*, appeared in 1623 and is an expanded, Latinized version of the *Advancement of Learning* (the first really important philosophical book to be written in

Francis Bacon, oil painting by an unknown artist. In the National Portrait Gallery, London. Courtesy of the National Portrait Gallery, London

English). The *De Augmentis Scientiarum* contains a division of the sciences, a project that had not been embarked on to any great purpose since Aristotle and, in a smaller way, since the Stoics. The second part of Bacon's scheme, the *Novum Organum,* which had already appeared in 1620, gives "true directions concerning the interpretation of nature"—in other words, an account of the correct method of acquiring natural knowledge. This is what Bacon believed to be his most important contribution and is the body of ideas with which his name is most closely associated. The fields of possible knowledge having been charted in *De Augmentis Scientiarum,* the proper method for their cultivation was set out in *Novum Organum.*

Third, there is natural history, the register of matters of observed natural fact, which is the indispensable raw material for the inductive method. Bacon wrote "histories," in this sense, of the wind, life and death, and the dense as well as the rare. Near the end of his life he was working on his *Sylva Sylvarum: Or A Natural Historie* ("Forest of Forests"), in effect, a collection of collections, a somewhat uncritical miscellany.

Fourth, there is the "ladder of the intellect," consisting of thoroughly formulated examples of the Baconian method in application, the most successful one being the exemplary account in *Novum Organum* of how his inductive "tables" show heat to be a kind of motion of particles. (Bacon distinguished three kinds of such tables: tables of presence, absence, and degree—i.e., in the case of any two properties, such as heat and friction, instances in which they appear together, instances in which one appears without the other, and instances in which their amounts vary proportionately. The ultimate purpose of these tables was to order facts in such a way that the true causes of phenomena [the subject of physics] and the true "forms" of things [the subject of metaphysics—the study of the nature of being] could be inductively established.)

Fifth, there are the "forerunners," or pieces of scientific knowledge arrived at by pre-Baconian, commonsense methods. Sixth and finally, there is the new philosophy, or science itself, seen by Bacon as a task for later generations armed with his method, advancing into all the regions of possible discovery set out in the *Advancement of Learning*. The wonder is not so much that Bacon did not complete this immense design but that he got as far with it as he did.

THE IDOLS OF THE MIND

In the first book of *Novum Organum*, Bacon discusses the causes of human error in the pursuit of knowledge. Aristotle had discussed logical fallacies, commonly found in human reasoning, but Bacon was original in looking behind the forms of reasoning to underlying psychological causes. He invented the metaphor of "idol" to refer to such causes of human error.

Bacon distinguishes four idols, or main varieties of proneness to error. The idols of the tribe are certain intellectual faults that are universal to humankind, or, at any rate, particularly common. One, for example, is a tendency toward oversimplification—that is, supposing, for the sake of tidiness, that there exists more order in a field of inquiry than there actually is. Another is a propensity to be overly influenced by particularly sudden or exciting occurrences that are in fact unrepresentative.

The idols of the cave are the intellectual peculiarities of individuals. One person may concentrate on the likenesses, another on the differences, between things. One may fasten on detail, another on the totality.

The idols of the marketplace are the kinds of error for which language is responsible. It has always been a distinguishing feature of English philosophy to emphasize the unreliable nature of language, which is seen, nominalistically, as a human improvisation. Nominalists argue that even if the power of speech is given by God, it was Adam who named the beasts and thereby gave that power its concrete realization. But language, like other human achievements, partakes of human imperfections. Bacon was particularly concerned with the superficiality of distinctions drawn in everyday language, by which things fundamentally different are classed together (whales and fishes as fish, for example) and things fundamentally similar are distinguished (ice, water, and steam). But he was also concerned, like later critics of language, with the capacity of words to embroil people in the discussion of the meaningless (as, for example, in discussions of the deity Fortune). This aspect of Bacon's thought has been almost as influential as his account of natural knowledge, inspiring a long tradition of skeptical rationalism, from the Enlightenment to the positivism of the 19th century and the logical positivism of the 20th century.

The fourth and final group of idols is that of the idols of the theatre, that is to say mistaken systems of philosophy in the broadest, Baconian sense of the term, in which it embraces all beliefs of any degree of generality. Bacon's critical polemic in discussing the idols of the theatre is lively but not philosophically penetrating. He speaks, for example, of the vain affectations of the humanists, but they were not an apt subject for his criticism. Humanists were really anti-philosophers who not unreasonably turned their attention to nonphilosophical matters because of the apparent inability of philosophers to arrive at conclusions that were either generally agreed upon or useful. Bacon does have something to say about the skeptical philosophy to which humanists appealed when they felt the need for it. Insofar as skepticism involves doubts about deductive reasoning, he has no quarrel with it. Insofar as it is applied not to reason but to the ability of the senses to supply the reason with reliable premises to work from, he brushes it aside too easily.

Bacon's attack on Scholastic orthodoxy is surprisingly rhetorical. It may be that he supposed it to be already sufficiently discredited by its incurably contentious or disputatious character. In his view it was a largely verbal technique for the indefinite prolongation of inconclusive argument by the drawing of artificial distinctions. He has some awareness of the central weakness of Aristotelian science, namely its attempt to derive substantial conclusions from premises that are intuitively evident, and argues that the apparently obvious axioms are neither clear nor indisputable. Perhaps Bacon's most fruitful disagreement with Scholasticism is his belief that natural knowledge is cumulative, a process of discovery, not of conservation. Living in a time when new worlds were being found on Earth, he was able to free himself from the view that everything people needed to know had already been revealed in the Bible or by Aristotle.

Against the fantastic learning of the occultists Bacon argued that individual reports are insufficient, especially because people are emotionally predisposed to credit the interestingly strange. Observations worthy to substantiate theories must be repeatable. Bacon defended the study of nature against those who considered it as either base or dangerous. He argued for a cooperative and methodical procedure and against individualism and intuition.

THE NEW METHOD

The core of Bacon's philosophy of science is the account of inductive reasoning given in Book II of *Novum Organum*. The defect of all previous systems of beliefs about nature, he argued, lay in the inadequate treatment of the general propositions from which the deductions were made.

Either they were the result of precipitate generalization from one or two cases, or they were uncritically assumed to be self-evident on the basis of their familiarity and general acceptance.

To avoid hasty generalization Bacon urges a technique of "gradual ascent," that is, the patient accumulation of well-founded generalizations of steadily increasing degrees of generality. This method would have the benefit of freeing people's minds from ill-constructed everyday concepts that obliterate important differences and fail to register important similarities.

The crucial point, Bacon realized, is that induction must work by elimination not, as it does in common life and the defective scientific tradition, by simple enumeration. Thus he stressed "the greater force of the negative instance": the fact that while "all As are Bs" is only weakly confirmed by "this A is a B," it is shown conclusively to be false by "this A is not a B." His tables were formal devices for the presentation of singular pieces of evidence to facilitate the rapid discovery of false generalizations. What survives this eliminative screening, Bacon assumes, may be taken to be true.

The conception of a scientific research establishment, which Bacon developed in his utopia, *The New Atlantis*, may be a more important contribution to science than his theory of induction. Here the idea of science as a collaborative undertaking, conducted in an impersonally methodical fashion and animated by the intention to give material benefits to mankind, is set out with literary force.

THE MATERIALISM OF THOMAS HOBBES

Thomas Hobbes was acquainted with both Bacon and Galileo. With the first he shared a strong concern for philosophical method, with the second an overwhelming interest in matter in motion. His philosophical efforts, however, were more inclusive and more complete than those of his contemporaries. He was a comprehensive thinker within the scope of an exceedingly narrow set of presuppositions, and he produced one of the most systematic philosophies of the early modern period: an almost completely consistent description of humankind, civil society, and nature according to the tenets of mechanistic materialism.

Hobbes's account of what philosophy is and ought to be clearly distinguished between content and method. As method, philosophy is simply reasoning or calculating by the use of words as to the causes or effects of phenomena. When a person reasons from causes to effects, he reasons synthetically; when he reasons from effects to causes, he reasons analytically. (Hobbes's strong inclination toward deduction and geometric proofs favoured arguments of the former type.) His dogmatic metaphysical assumption was that physical reality consists entirely of matter in motion. The real world is a corporeal universe in constant movement, and phenomena, or events, the causes and effects of which it is the business of philosophy to lay bare, consist of either the action of physical bodies on each other or the quaint effects of physical bodies upon minds. From this assumption follows Hobbes's classification of the fields that form the content of philosophy: (1) physics, (2) moral philosophy, and (3) civil philosophy. Physics is the science of the motions and actions of physical bodies conceived in terms of cause and effect. Moral philosophy (or, more accurately, psychology) is the detailed study of "the passions and perturbations of the mind"— that is, how minds are "moved" by desire, aversion, appetite, fear, anger, and envy. And civil philosophy deals with the concerted actions of people in a common-wealth—how, in detail, the wayward wills of human beings can be constrained by power (i.e., force) to prevent civil disorder and maintain peace.

Hobbes's philosophy was a bold restatement of Greek atomistic materialism, with applications to the realities of early modern politics that would have seemed strange to its ancient authors. But there are also elements in it that make it characteristically English. Hobbes's account of language led him to adopt nominalism and deny the reality of universals. (A *universal* is a quality or property that each individual member of a class of things must possess if the same general word is to apply to all the things in that class. Redness, for example, is a universal possessed by all red objects.) The *problem of universals* is the question of whether universals are concepts, verbal expressions, or a special kind of entity that exists independently, outside space and time. Bacon's general emphasis on experience also had its analogue in Hobbes's theory that all knowledge arises from sense experiences, all of which are caused by the actions of physical bodies on the sense organs. Empiricism has been a basic and recurrent feature of British intellectual life, and its nominalist and sensationalist roots were already clearly evident in both Bacon and Hobbes.

HOBBES'S SYSTEM

Theories that trace all observed effects to matter and motion are called mechanical. Hobbes was thus a mechanical materialist: he held that nothing but material things are real, and he thought that the subject matter of all the natural sciences consists of the motions of material things at different levels of generality. Geometry considers the effects of the motions of points, lines, and solids; pure mechanics deals with the motions of three-dimensional bodies in a full space, or plenum; physics deals with the motions of the parts of inanimate bodies insofar as they contribute to observed phenomena; and psychology deals with the effects of the internal motions of animate bodies on behaviour. The system of the natural sciences described in Hobbes's trilogy represents his understanding of the materialist principles on which all science is based.

The fact that Hobbes included politics as well as psychology within his system, however, has tended to overshadow his insistence on the autonomy of political understanding from natural-scientific understanding. According to Hobbes, politics need not need be understood in terms of the motions of material things (although, ultimately, it can be). A certain kind of widely available self-knowledge is evidence enough of the human propensity to war. Although Hobbes is routinely read as having discerned the "laws of motion" for both human beings and human societies, the most that can plausibly be claimed is that he based his political philosophy on psychological principles that he thought could be illuminated by general laws of motion.

POLITICAL PHILOSOPHY

Hobbes presented his political philosophy in different forms for different audiences. *De Cive* states his theory in what he regarded as its most scientific form. Unlike *The Elements of Law*, which was composed in English for English parliamentarians — and written with local political challenges to Charles I in mind — *De Cive* was a Latin work for an audience of Continental savants who were interested in the "new" science: the sort of science that did not appeal to the authority of the ancients but approached various problems with fresh principles of explanation.

De Cive's break from the ancient authority par excellence—Aristotle—could not have been more loudly advertised. After only a few paragraphs, Hobbes rejects one of the most famous theses of Aristotle's politics, namely that human beings are naturally suited to life in a polis and do not fully realize their natures until they exercise the role of citizen. Hobbes turns Aristotle's claim on its head: human beings, he insists, are by nature unsuited to political life. They naturally denigrate and compete with each other, are quite easily swayed by the rhetoric of ambitious men, and think much more highly of themselves than of other people. In short, their passions magnify the value they place on their own interests, especially their near-term interests. At the same time, most people, in pursuing their own interests, do not have the ability to prevail over competitors. Nor can they appeal to some natural common standard of behaviour that everyone will feel obliged to respect. There is no natural self-restraint, even when human beings are moderate in their appetites, for a ruthless and bloodthirsty few can make even the moderate feel forced to take violent preemptive action to avoid losing everything. The self-restraint even of the moderate, then, easily turns into aggression. In other words, no human being is above aggression and the anarchy that goes with it.

War comes more naturally to human beings than political order. Indeed, political order is possible only when human beings abandon their natural condition of judging and pursuing what seems best to each and delegate this judgment to someone else. This delegation is effected when the many contract together to submit to a sovereign in return for physical safety and a modicum of well-being. Each of the many essentially says to the other: "I transfer my right of governing myself to X (the sovereign) if you do too." And the transfer is collectively entered into only on the understanding that it makes one less of a target of attack or dispossession than one would be in one's natural state. Although Hobbes did not assume that there was ever a real historical event in which a mutual promise was made to delegate self-government to a sovereign, he claimed that the best way to understand the state was to conceive of it as having resulted from such an agreement.

In Hobbes's social contract, the many trade liberty for safety. Liberty, with its standing invitation to local conflict and finally all-out war—a "war of every man against every man"—is overvalued in traditional political philosophy and popular opinion, according to Hobbes. It is better for people to transfer the right of governing themselves to the sovereign. Once transferred, however, this right of government is absolute, unless the many feel that their lives are threatened by submission. The sovereign determines who owns what, who will hold which public offices, how the economy will be regulated, what acts will be crimes, and what punishments criminals should receive. The sovereign is the supreme commander of the army, supreme interpreter of law, and supreme interpreter of scripture, with authority over any national church. It is unjust—a case of reneging on what one has agreed—for any subject to take issue with these arrangements, for, in the act of creating the state or by receiving its protection, one agrees to leave judgments about the means of collective well-being and security to the sovereign. The sovereign's laws and decrees and appointments to public office may be unpopular, and they may even be wrong. But unless the sovereign fails so utterly that subjects feel that their condition would be no worse in the free-for-all outside the state, it is better for the subjects to endure the sovereign's rule.

It is better both prudentially and morally. Because no one can prudently welcome a greater risk of death, no one

In Hobbes's social contract, the many exchange liberty for safety, and a sovereign (Queen Elizabeth I, for instance, illustrated here) wields absolute power.
Hulton Archive/Getty Images

can prudently prefer total liberty to submission. Total liberty invites war, and submission is the best insurance against war. Morality too supports this conclusion, for, according to Hobbes, all the moral precepts enjoining virtuous behaviour can be understood as derivable from the fundamental moral precept that one should seek peace—that is to say, freedom from war—if it is safe to do so. Without peace, he observed, man lives in "continual fear, and danger of violent death," and what life he has is "solitary, poor, nasty, brutish, and short." What Hobbes calls the "laws of nature," the system of moral rules by which everyone is bound, cannot be safely complied with outside the state, for the total liberty that people have outside the state includes the liberty to flout the moral requirements if one's survival seems to depend on it.

The sovereign is not a party to the social contract. He receives the obedience of the many as a free gift in their hope that he will see to their safety. The sovereign makes no promises to the many to win their submission. Indeed, because he does not transfer his right of self-government to anyone, he retains the total liberty that his subjects trade for safety. He is not bound by law, including his own laws. Nor does he do anything unjustly if he makes decisions about his subjects's safety and well-being that they do not like.

Although the sovereign is in a position to judge the means of survival and well-being for the many more dispassionately than they are able to do themselves, he is not immune to self-interested passions. Hobbes realizes that the sovereign may behave iniquitously. He insists that it is utterly imprudent for a sovereign to act so unjustly that he disappoints his subjects's expectation of safety and makes them feel insecure. Subjects who are in fear of their lives lose their obligations to obey and, with that, deprive the sovereign of his power. Reduced to the status of one among many by the defection of his subjects, the unseated sovereign is likely to feel the wrath of those who submitted to him in vain.

Hobbes's masterpiece, *Leviathan* (1651), does not significantly depart from the view of *De Cive* concerning the relation between protection and obedience, but it devotes much more attention to the civil obligations of Christian believers and the proper and improper roles of a church within a state. Hobbes argues that believers do not endanger their prospects of salvation by obeying a sovereign's decrees to the letter, and he maintains that churches do not have any authority that is not granted by the civil sovereign.

THE RATIONALISM OF RENÉ DESCARTES

The dominant philosophy of the last half of the 17th century was that of the French rationalist thinker René Descartes. A crucial figure in the history of philosophy, Descartes combined (however unconsciously or even unwillingly) the influences of the past into a synthesis that was striking in its originality and yet congenial to the scientific temper of the age. In the minds of all later historians, he counts as the progenitor of the modern spirit of philosophy.

Each of the maxims of Leonardo da Vinci, which constitute the Renaissance worldview, found its place in Descartes: empiricism in the physiological researches described in the *Discours de la méthode* (1637; *Discourse on Method*); a mechanistic interpretation of the physical world and of human action in the *Principia Philosophiae* (1644; *Principles of Philosophy*) and Les Passions de l'âme (1649; *The Passions of the Soul*); and a mathematical bias that dominates the theory of method in *Regulae ad*

Lauded as the father of the modern philosophy, René Descartes amalgamated influences of the past with the more scientific constitution of the day. Hulton Archive/Getty Images

Directionem Ingenii (*Rules for the Direction of the Mind*), published posthumously in 1701; and the metaphysics of the *Meditationes de Prima Philosophia* (1641; *Meditations on the First Philosophy*). But it is the mathematical theme that clearly predominates in Descartes's philosophy. From the past there seeped into the Cartesian synthesis doctrines about God from Anselm of Canterbury (*c.* 1033–1109) and Thomas Aquinas, a theory of the will from Augustine, a deep sympathy with the Stoicism of the Romans, and a skeptical method taken indirectly from Pyrrhon of Elis (*c.* 360–*c.* 272 BCE) and Sextus

Empiricus. But Descartes was also a great mathematician—he invented analytic geometry—and the author of many important physical and anatomical experiments. He knew and profoundly respected the work of Galileo. Indeed, he withdrew from publication his own cosmological treatise, *Le Monde* (*The World*), after Galileo's condemnation by the Inquisition in 1633.

Descartes's System

Bacon and Descartes, the founders of modern empiricism and rationalism, respectively, both subscribed to two pervasive tenets of the Renaissance: an enormous enthusiasm for physical science and the belief that knowledge means power—that the ultimate purpose of theoretical science is to serve the practical needs of human beings.

In his *Principles*, Descartes defined philosophy as "the study of wisdom" or "the perfect knowledge of all one can know." Its chief utility is "for the conduct of life" (morals), "the conservation of health" (medicine), and "the invention of all the arts" (mechanics). Using the famous metaphor of the "tree," he expressed the relation of philosophy to practical endeavours: the roots are metaphysics; the trunk is physics; and the branches are morals, medicine, and mechanics. The metaphor is revealing, because it indicates that for Descartes—as for Bacon and Galileo—the most important part of the tree was the trunk. In other words, Descartes busied himself with metaphysics only to provide a firm foundation for physics. Thus, the *Discourse on Method*, which provides a synoptic view of the Cartesian philosophy, shows it to be not a metaphysics founded on physics (as was the case with Aristotle) but rather a physics founded on metaphysics.

Descartes's mathematical bias was reflected in his determination to ground natural science not in sensation and probability (as did Bacon) but in premises that could be known with absolute certainty. Thus his metaphysics in essence consisted of three principles:

1. To employ the procedure of complete and systematic doubt to eliminate every belief that does not pass the test of indubitability (skepticism).
2. To accept no idea as certain that is not clear, distinct, and free of contradiction (mathematicism).
3. To found all knowledge upon the bedrock certainty of self-consciousness, so that "I think, therefore I am" becomes the only innate idea unshakable by doubt (subjectivism).

From the indubitability of the self, Descartes inferred the existence of a perfect God. From the fact that a perfect being is incapable of falsification or deception, he concluded that the ideas about the physical world that God has implanted in human beings must be true. The achievement of certainty about the natural world was thus guaranteed by the perfection of God and by the "clear and distinct" ideas that are his gift.

Cartesian metaphysics is the fountainhead of rationalism in modern philosophy, for it suggests that the mathematical criteria of clarity, distinctness, and logical consistency are the ultimate test of meaningfulness and truth. This stance is profoundly antiempirical. Bacon, who remarked that "reasoners resemble spiders who make cobwebs out of their own substance," might well have said the same of Descartes, for the Cartesian self is just such a substance. Yet for Descartes the understanding is vastly superior to the senses, and only reason can ultimately decide what constitutes truth in science.

Cartesianism dominated the intellectual life of continental Europe until the end of the 17th century. It was a fashionable philosophy, appealing to learned gentlemen and highborn ladies alike, and it was one of the few philosophical alternatives to the Scholasticism still being taught in the universities. Precisely for this reason it constituted a serious threat to established religious authority. In 1663 the Roman Catholic Church placed Descartes's works on the *Index Librorum Prohibitorum* ("Index of Forbidden Books"), and the University of Oxford forbade the teaching of his doctrines. Only in the liberal Dutch universities, such as those of Groningen and Utrecht, did Cartesianism make serious headway.

Certain features of Cartesian philosophy made it an important starting point for subsequent philosophical speculation. As a kind of meeting point for medieval and modern worldviews, it accepted the doctrines of Renaissance science while attempting to ground them metaphysically in medieval notions of God and the human mind. Thus, a certain dualism between God the Creator and the mechanistic world of his creation, between mind as a spiritual principle and matter as mere spatial extension, was inherent in the Cartesian position. An entire generation of Cartesians—among them Arnold Geulincx (1624–69), Nicolas Malebranche (1638–1715), and Pierre Bayle (1647–1706)—wrestled with the resulting problem of how interaction between two such radically different entities is possible.

MEDITATIONS

Descartes's *Meditations on First Philosophy* was written in Latin and dedicated to the Jesuit professors at the Sorbonne in Paris. The work includes critical responses by several eminent thinkers—collected by the French theologian and mathematician Marin Mersenne (1588–1648) from the French philosopher and theologian Antoine Arnauld (1612–94), Thomas Hobbes (1588–1679), and the Epicurean atomist Pierre Gassendi (1592–1655)—as well as Descartes's replies. The second edition (1642) includes a response by the Jesuit priest Pierre Bourdin (1595–1653), who Descartes said was a fool. These objections and replies constitute a landmark of cooperative discussion in philosophy and science at a time when dogmatism was the rule.

The *Meditations* is characterized by Descartes's use of methodic doubt, a systematic procedure of rejecting as though false all types of belief in which one has ever been, or could ever be, deceived. His arguments derive from the skepticism of Sextus Empiricus as reflected in the work of the Michel de Montaigne and the Catholic theologian Pierre Charron (1541–1603). Thus, Descartes's apparent knowledge based on authority is set aside, because even experts are sometimes wrong. His beliefs from sensory experience are declared untrustworthy, because such experience is sometimes misleading, as when a square tower appears round from a distance. Even his beliefs about the objects in his immediate vicinity may be mistaken, because, as he notes, he often has dreams about objects that do not exist, and he has no way of knowing with certainty whether he is dreaming or awake. Finally, his apparent knowledge of simple and general truths of reasoning that do not depend on sense experience (such as "$2 + 3 = 5$" or "a square has four sides") is also unreliable, because God could have made him in such a way that, for example, he goes wrong every time he counts. As a way of summarizing the universal doubt into which he has fallen, Descartes supposes that an "evil genius of the utmost power and cunning has employed all his energies in order to deceive me."

Although at this stage there is seemingly no belief about which he cannot entertain doubt, Descartes finds certainty in the intuition that when he is thinking (even if he is being deceived), he must exist. In the *Discourse*, Descartes expresses this intuition in the dictum "I think, therefore I am." Because "therefore" suggests that the intuition is an argument (though it is not) in the *Meditations* he says merely, "I think, I am" ("Cogito, sum"). The cogito is a logically self-evident truth that also gives intuitively certain knowledge of a particular thing's existence—that is, one's self. Nevertheless, it justifies accepting as certain only the existence of the person who thinks it. If all one ever knew for certain was that one exists, and if one adhered to Descartes's method of doubting all that is uncertain, one would be reduced to solipsism, the view that nothing exists but one's self and thoughts. To escape solipsism, Descartes argues that all ideas that are as "clear and distinct" as the cogito must be true, for, if they were not, the cogito also, as a member of the class of clear and distinct ideas, could be doubted. Because "I think, I am" cannot be doubted, all clear and distinct ideas must be true.

On the basis of clear and distinct innate ideas, Descartes then establishes that each mind is a mental substance and each body a part of one material substance. The mind or soul is immortal, because it is unextended and cannot be broken into parts, as can extended bodies. Descartes also advances a proof for the existence of God. He begins with the proposition that he has an innate idea of God as a perfect being and then concludes that God necessarily exists, because, if he did not, he would not be perfect. This ontological argument for God's existence, originally due to Anselm, is at the heart of Descartes's rationalism, because it establishes certain knowledge about an existing thing solely on the basis of reasoning from innate ideas, with no help from sensory experience.

Descartes then argues that, because God is perfect, he does not deceive human beings; and therefore, because God leads us to believe that the material world exists, it does exist. In this way Descartes claims to establish metaphysical foundations for the existence of his own mind, of God, and of the material world.

The inherent circularity of Descartes's reasoning was exposed by Arnauld, whose objection has come to be known as the Cartesian Circle. According to Descartes, God's existence is established by the fact that Descartes has a clear and distinct idea of God. But the truth of Descartes's clear and distinct ideas are guaranteed by the fact that God exists and is not a deceiver. Thus, to show that God exists, Descartes must assume that God exists.

THE RATIONALISM OF BENEDICT DE SPINOZA

The tradition of Continental rationalism was carried on by two philosophers of genius: the Dutch Jewish philosopher Benedict de Spinoza and his younger contemporary Gottfried Wilhelm Leibniz. Whereas Bacon's philosophy had been a search for method in science and Descartes's basic aim had been the achievement of scientific certainty, Spinoza's speculative system was one of the most comprehensive of the early modern period. In certain respects Spinoza had much in common with Hobbes: a mechanistic worldview and even a political philosophy that sought political stability in centralized power. Yet Spinoza introduced a conception of philosophizing that was new to the Renaissance; philosophy became a personal and moral quest for wisdom and the achievement of human perfection.

Spinoza's magnum opus, the *Ethica* (*Ethics*), published posthumously in 1677, is written as a geometric proof in the style of Euclid (flourished *c.* 300 BCE). Spinoza apparently believed that a geometric presentation of his ideas would be clearer than the conventional narrative style of his earlier works. Accordingly, he begins with a set of definitions of key terms and a series of self-evident "axioms" and proceeds to derive from these a number of "theorems," or propositions. The early portion of the work contains no introductory or explanatory material to aid the reader, apparently because Spinoza initially thought it unnecessary. By the middle of Part I, however, he had added various notes and observations to ensure that the reader would understand the significance of the conclusions being developed. By the end of Part I, he had also added polemical essays and introductions to various topics. The form of the work as a whole is therefore a mixture of axiomatic proof and philosophical narrative.

Spinoza begins by stating a set of definitions of eight terms: *self-caused, finite of its own kind, substance, attribute, mode, God, freedom*, and *eternity*. These definitions are followed by a series of axioms, one of which supposedly guarantees that the results of Spinoza's logical demonstrations will be true about reality. Spinoza quickly establishes that substance must be existent, self-caused, and unlimited. From this he proves that there cannot be two substances with the same attribute, because each would limit the other. This leads to the monumental conclusion of Proposition 11: "God, or substance consisting of infinite attributes, each of which expresses eternal and infinite essence, necessarily exists." From the definition of God as a substance with infinite attributes and other propositions about substance, it follows that "there can be, or be conceived, no other substance but God" (Proposition 14) and that "whatever is, is in God, and nothing can be or be conceived without God" (Proposition 15). This constitutes the core of Spinoza's pantheism: God

is everywhere, and everything that exists is a modification
of God. God is known by human beings through only
two of his attributes—thought and extension (the quality
of having spatial dimensions)—though the number of
God's attributes is infinite. Later in Part I, Spinoza established that everything that occurs necessarily follows
from the nature of God and that there can be no contingencies in nature. Part I concludes with an appended
polemic about the misreading of the world by religious
and superstitious people who think that God can change
the course of events and that the course of events sometimes reflects a divine judgment of human behaviour.

Part II explores the two attributes through which
human beings understand the world, thought and extension. The latter form of understanding is developed in
natural science, the former in logic and psychology. For
Spinoza, there is no problem, as there is for Descartes, of
explaining the interaction between mind and body. The
two are not distinct entities causally interacting with each
other but merely different aspects of the same events.

Spinoza accepted the mechanistic physics of Descartes
as the right way of understanding the world in terms of
extension. Individual physical or mental entities are
"modes" of substance: physical entities are modes of substance understood in terms of the attribute of extension,
and mental entities are modes of substance understood in
terms of the attribute of thought. Because God is the only
substance, all physical and mental entities are modes of
God. Modes are *natura naturata* ("nature-created") and
transitory, whereas God, or substance, is *natura naturans*
("nature-creating") and eternal.

Physical modes that are biological have a feature
beyond simple extension, namely, *conatus* (Latin: "exer-
tion" or "effort"), a desire and drive for self-preservation.
Unconsciously, biological modes are also driven by

emotions of fear and pleasure to act in certain ways. Human beings, as biological modes, are in a state of bondage as long as they act solely from emotions. In Part V of the *Ethics*, "Of Human Freedom," Spinoza explains that freedom is achieved by understanding the power of the emotions over human actions, rationally accepting things and events over which one has no control, and increasing one's knowledge and cultivating one's intellect. The highest form of knowledge consists of an intellectual intuition of things in their existence as modes and attributes of eternal substance, or God, which is what it means to see the world from the aspect of eternity. This kind of knowledge leads to a deeper understanding of God, who is all things, and ultimately to an intellectual love of God (*amor Dei intellectualis*), a form of blessedness amounting to a kind of rational-mystical experience.

THE RATIONALISM OF GOTTFRIED WILHELM LEIBNIZ

Whereas the basic elements of the Spinozistic worldview are given in the *Ethics*, Leibniz's philosophy must be pieced together from numerous brief expositions, which seem to be mere philosophical interludes in an otherwise busy life. But the philosophical form is deceptive. Leibniz was a mathematician (he and Isaac Newton independently invented the infinitesimal calculus), jurist (he codified the laws of Mainz, Ger.), diplomat, historian to royalty, and court librarian in a princely house. Yet he was also one of the most original philosophers of the early modern period.

His chief contributions were in the fields of logic, in which he was a truly brilliant innovator, and metaphysics, in which he provided a rationalist alternative to the philosophies of Descartes and Spinoza. Leibniz conceived of logic as a mathematical calculus. He was the first to

Voltaire's novel Candide *soundly and satirically spurned Leibniz's heedlessly sanguine worldview.* AFP/Getty Images

MODERN PHILOSOPHY: FROM 1500 CE TO THE PRESENT

distinguish "truths of reason" from "truths of fact" and to contrast the necessary propositions of logic and mathematics, which hold in all "possible worlds," with the contingent propositions of science, which hold only in some possible worlds (including the actual world). He saw clearly that, as the first kind of proposition is governed by the principle of contradiction (a proposition and its negation cannot both be true), the second is governed by the principle of sufficient reason (nothing exists or is the case without a sufficient reason). This principle was the basis of Leibniz's claim that the actual world is the "best of all possible worlds" that God could have created: his choice of this world over the others required a sufficient reason, which, for Leibniz, was the fact that this world was the best, despite the existence of evident evils. Any other possible world would have had evils of its own sort of even greater magnitude. (Leibniz's blindly optimistic view of the world was satirically rejected in the novel *Candide* [1759] by Voltaire [1694–1788].)

In metaphysics, Leibniz's pluralism contrasted with Descartes's dualism and Spinoza's monism. Leibniz posited the existence of an infinite number of spiritual substances, which he called "monads," each different, each a percipient of the universe around it, and each mirroring that universe from its own point of view. However, the differences between Leibniz's philosophy and that of Descartes and Spinoza are less significant than their similarities, in particular their extreme rationalism. In the *Principes de la nature et de la grâce fondés en raison* (1714; "Principles of Nature and of Grace Founded in Reason"), Leibniz stated a maxim that could fairly represent the entire school:

True reasoning depends upon necessary or eternal truths, such as those of logic, numbers, geometry, which establish an indubitable connection of ideas and unfailing consequences.

CHAPTER 3

PHILOSOPHY IN THE ENLIGHTENMENT

The European Enlightenment was an intellectual movement of the 17th and 18th centuries in which ideas concerning God, reason, nature, and humanity were synthesized into a worldview that gained wide assent and instigated revolutionary developments in art, philosophy, and politics. Central to Enlightenment thought were the use and celebration of reason, the power by which humans understand the universe and improve their own condition. The goals of rational man were considered to be knowledge, freedom, and happiness.

SOURCES AND DEVELOPMENT OF ENLIGHTENMENT THOUGHT

The powers and uses of reason had first been explored by the philosophers of ancient Greece, who discerned in the ordered regularity of nature the workings of an intelligent mind. Rome adopted and preserved much of Greek culture, notably including the ideas of a rational natural order and natural law. Amid the turmoil of empire, however, a new concern arose for personal salvation, and the way was paved for the triumph of the Christian religion. Christian thinkers gradually found uses for their Greco-Roman heritage. The system of thought known as Scholasticism, culminating in the work of Thomas Aquinas, resurrected reason as a tool of understanding but subordinated it to spiritual revelation and the revealed truths of Christianity.

The intellectual and political edifice of Christianity, seemingly impregnable in the Middle Ages, fell in turn to the assaults made on it by humanism, the Renaissance, and the Protestant Reformation. Humanism bred the experimental science of Bacon, Copernicus, and Galileo and the mathematical rigour of Descartes, Leibniz, and Newton. The Renaissance rediscovered much of Classical culture and revived the notion of humans as creative beings, while the Reformation, more directly but in the long run no less effectively, challenged the monolithic authority of the Roman Catholic Church. For the German Reformer Martin Luther as for Bacon or Descartes, the way to truth lay in the application of human reason. Received authority, whether of Ptolemy (*c.* 100–*c.* 170 CE), the originator of the Earth-centred model of the universe, in the sciences or of the church in matters of the spirit, was to be subject to the probings of unfettered minds.

The successful application of reason to any question depended on its correct application—on the development of a methodology of reasoning that would serve as its own guarantee of validity. Such a methodology was most spectacularly achieved in the sciences and mathematics, where the logics of induction and deduction made possible the creation of a sweeping new cosmology. The success of Newton, in particular, in capturing in a few mathematical equations the laws that govern the motions of the planets gave great impetus to a growing faith in the human capacity to attain knowledge. At the same time, the idea of the universe as a mechanism governed by a few simple (and discoverable) laws had a subversive effect on the concepts of a personal God and individual salvation that were central to Christianity.

Humanism led the likes of scientists such as Isaac Newton to foster experimentation in the Enlightenment. Hulton Archive/Getty Images

Inevitably, the method of reason was applied to religion itself. The product of a search for a natural—rational—religion was Deism, which, although never an organized cult or movement, conflicted with Christianity for two centuries, especially in England and France. For the Deist a small number of religious truths sufficed, and they were truths felt to be manifest to all rational beings: the existence of one God, often conceived of as architect or mechanician, the existence of a system of rewards and punishments administered by that God, and the obligation to be virtuous and pious. Beyond the natural religion of the Deists lay the more radical products of the application of reason to religion: skepticism, atheism, and materialism.

The Enlightenment produced the first modern secularized theories of psychology and ethics. The English empiricist John Locke (1632–1704) conceived of the human mind as being at birth a "tabula rasa," a blank slate on which experience wrote freely and boldly, creating individual character according to the individual's experience of the world. Supposed innate qualities, such as goodness or original sin, had no reality. In a darker vein, Hobbes portrayed humans as moved solely by considerations of their own pleasure and pain. The notion of humans as neither good nor bad but interested principally in survival and the maximization of pleasure led to radical political theories. Where the state had once been viewed as an earthly approximation of an eternal order, with the City of Man modeled on the City of God, now it came to be seen as a mutually beneficial arrangement, among individuals, conceived as a social contract, aimed at protecting the natural rights and self-interest of each.

This conception of society, however, contrasted sharply with the realities of actual societies. Thus the Enlightenment became critical, reforming, and eventually revolutionary. Locke and Jeremy Bentham (1748–1832)) in England, Jean-Jacques Rousseau (1712–78), Montesquieu (1689–1755), and Voltaire in France, and Thomas Jefferson (1743–1826) in America all contributed to an evolving critique of the arbitrary, authoritarian state and to sketching the outline of a higher form of social organization, based on natural rights and functioning as a political democracy. Such powerful ideas found expression as reform in England and as revolution in France (1789) and America (1775–83).

The Enlightenment expired as the victim of its own excesses. The more rarefied the religion of the Deists became, the less it offered those who sought solace or salvation. The celebration of abstract reason provoked contrary spirits to begin exploring the world of sensation and emotion in the cultural movement known as Romanticism. The Reign of Terror that followed the French Revolution severely tested the belief that people could govern themselves. The high optimism that marked much of Enlightenment thought, however, survived as one of the movement's most enduring legacies: the belief that human history is a record of general moral and intellectual progress.

CLASSICAL BRITISH EMPIRICISM

Although they both lived and worked in the late 17th century, Isaac Newton and John Locke were arguably the true fathers of the Enlightenment. Newton was the last of the scientific geniuses of the age, and his great *Philosophiae Naturalis Principia Mathematica* (1687; *Mathematical Principles of Natural Philosophy*) was the culmination of the movement that had begun with Copernicus and Galileo — the first scientific synthesis based on the application of mathematics to nature in every detail. The basic idea of the authority and autonomy of reason, which dominated all philosophizing in the 18th century, was, at bottom, the consequence of Newton's work.

Copernicus, Kepler, Bacon, Galileo, and Descartes, scientists and methodologists of science, performed like people urgently attempting to persuade nature to reveal its secrets. Newton's comprehensive mechanistic system made it seem as if at last nature had done so. It is impossible to exaggerate the enormous enthusiasm that this assumption kindled in all of the major thinkers of the late 17th and 18th centuries, from Locke to Kant. The new enthusiasm for reason that they all instinctively shared was based not on the mere advocacy of philosophers such as Descartes and Leibniz but on their conviction that, in the spectacular achievement of Newton, reason had succeeded in conquering the natural world.

Two major philosophical problems remained: to provide an account of the origins and extent of human knowledge and to shift the application of reason from the physical universe to human nature. The *Essay Concerning Human Understanding* (1690), by Locke, was devoted to the first, and the *Treatise of Human Nature* (1739–40), by the Scottish philosopher David Hume (1711–76)—"being an attempt to apply the method of experimental reasoning to moral subjects"—was devoted to the second.

These two basic tasks represented a new direction for philosophy since the late Renaissance. The Renaissance preoccupation with the natural world had constituted a certain "realistic" bias. Hobbes and Spinoza had each produced a metaphysics. They had been interested in the real constitution of the physical world. Moreover, the Renaissance enthusiasm for mathematics had resulted in a profound interest in rational principles, necessary propositions, and innate ideas. As attention was turned from the realities of nature to the structure of the mind that knows it so successfully, philosophers of the Enlightenment focused on the sensory and experiential components of knowledge rather than on the merely mathematical components. Thus, whereas the philosophy of the late Renaissance had been metaphysical and for the most part rationalistic, that of the Enlightenment was epistemological and empiricist. The school of British empiricism—whose major representatives are Locke, the Anglo-Irish philosopher George Berkeley (1685–1753), and Hume—dominated the perspective of Enlightenment philosophy until the time of Kant.

JOHN LOCKE

As mentioned earlier, whereas rationalist philosophers such as Descartes held that the ultimate source of human knowledge is reason, empiricists such as Locke argued that it is experience. Rationalist accounts of knowledge also typically involved the claim that at least some kinds of ideas are "innate," or present in the mind at (or even before) birth. For philosophers such as Descartes and Leibniz, the hypothesis of innateness is required to explain how humans come to have ideas of certain kinds. These ideas include not only mathematical concepts such as numbers, which appear not to be derived from sense experience, but also, according to some thinkers, certain general metaphysical principles, such as "every event has a cause."

Locke claimed that this line of argument has no force. He held that all ideas (except those that are "trifling") can be explained in terms of experience. Instead of attacking the doctrine of innate ideas directly, however, his strategy was to refute it by showing that it is explanatorily otiose and hence dispensable.

There are two kinds of experience, according to Locke: observation of external objects (i.e., sensation) and observation of the internal operations of the mind. Locke called this latter kind of experience, for which there is no natural word in English, "reflection." Some examples of reflection are perceiving, thinking, doubting, believing, reasoning, knowing, and willing.

As Locke uses the term, a "simple idea" is anything that is an "immediate object of perception" (i.e., an object as it is perceived by the mind) or anything that the mind "perceives *in itself*" through reflection. Simple ideas, whether they are ideas of perception or ideas of reflection, may be combined or repeated to produce "compound ideas," as when the compound idea of an apple is produced by bringing together simple ideas of a certain colour, texture, odour, and figure. Abstract ideas are created when "ideas taken from particular beings become general representatives of all of the same kind."

The "qualities" of an object are its powers to cause ideas in the mind. One consequence of this definition is that, in Locke's epistemology, words designating the sensible properties of objects are systematically ambiguous. The word *red,* for example, can mean either the idea of red in the mind or the quality in an object that causes that idea. Locke distinguished between primary and secondary qualities, as Galileo did. According to Locke, primary qualities, but not secondary qualities, are represented in the mind as they exist in the object itself. The primary qualities of an object, in other words, resemble the ideas they cause in the mind. Examples of primary qualities include "solidity, extension, figure, motion, or rest, and number." Secondary qualities are configurations or arrangements of primary qualities that cause sensible ideas such as sounds, colours, odours, and tastes. Thus, according to Locke's view, the phenomenal redness of a fire engine is not in the fire engine itself, but its phenomenal solidity is. Similarly, the phenomenal sweet odour of a rose is not in the rose itself, but its phenomenal extension is.

In Book IV of the *Essay Concerning Human Understanding*, Locke defines knowledge as "*the perception of the connexion of and agreement, or disagreement and repugnancy of any of our ideas.*" Knowledge so defined admits of three degrees, according to Locke. The first is what he calls "intuitive knowledge," in which the mind "perceives the agreement or disagreement of two ideas *immediately by themselves*, without the intervention of any other." Although Locke's first examples of intuitive knowledge are analytic propositions such as "*white* is not *black*," "a *circle* is not a *triangle*," and "*three* are more than *two*," later he says that "the knowledge of our own being we have by intuition." Relying on the metaphor of light as Augustine and others had, Locke says of this knowledge that "the mind is presently filled with the clear light of it. *It is on this intuition that depends all the certainty and evidence of all our knowledge.*"

The second degree of knowledge obtains when "the mind perceives the agreement or disagreement of...ideas, but not immediately." In these cases, some mediating idea makes it possible to see the connection between two other ideas. In a demonstration (or proof), for example, the connection between any premise and the conclusion is mediated by other premises and by the laws of logic. Demonstrative knowledge, although certain, is less certain than intuitive knowledge, according to Locke, because it requires effort and attention to go through the steps needed to recognize the certainty of the conclusion.

A third degree of knowledge, "sensitive knowledge," is roughly the same as what John Duns Scotus (*c.* 1266–1308) called "intuitive cognition," namely, the perception of "*the particular existence of finite beings without us.*" Unlike intuitive cognition, however, Locke's sensitive knowledge is not the most certain kind of knowledge it is possible to have. For him, it is less certain than intuitive or demonstrative knowledge.

Next in certainty to knowledge is probability, which Locke defines as the appearance of agreement or disagreement of ideas with each other. Like knowledge, probability admits of degrees, the highest of which attaches to propositions endorsed by the general consent of all people in all ages. Locke may have had in mind the virtually general consent of his contemporaries in the proposition that God exists, but he also explicitly mentions beliefs about causal relations.

The next-highest degree of probability belongs to propositions that hold not universally but for the most part, such as "people prefer their own private advantage to the public good." This sort of proposition is typically derived from history. A still lower degree of probability attaches to claims about specific facts, for example, that a man named Julius Caesar lived a long time ago. Problems arise when testimonies conflict, as they often do, but there is no simple rule or set of rules that determines how one ought to resolve such controversies.

Probability can concern not only objects of possible sense experience, as most of the foregoing examples do, but also things that are outside the sensible realm, such as angels, devils, magnetism, and molecules.

GEORGE BERKELEY

It was precisely this dualism of primary and secondary qualities that Locke's successor, George Berkeley, sought to overcome. Although Berkeley was a bishop in the Anglican church who professed a desire to combat atheistic materialism, his importance for the theory of knowledge lies rather in the way in which he demonstrated that, in the end, primary qualities are reducible to secondary qualities. His empiricism led to a denial of abstract ideas because he believed that general notions are simply fictions of the mind. Science, he argued, can easily dispense with the concept of matter: nature is simply that which human beings perceive through their sense faculties. This means that sense experiences themselves can be considered "objects for the mind." A physical object, therefore, is simply a recurrent group of sense qualities. With this important reduction of substance to quality, Berkeley became the father of the epistemological position known as phenomenalism.

In his major work, *Treatise Concerning the Principles of Human Knowledge* (1710), Berkeley asserted that nothing exists except ideas and spirits (minds or souls). He distinguished three kinds of ideas: those that come from sense experience correspond to Locke's simple ideas of perception; those that come from "attending to the passions and operations of the mind" correspond to Locke's ideas of reflection; and those that come from compounding, dividing, or otherwise representing ideas correspond to Locke's compound ideas. By "spirit" Berkeley meant "one simple, undivided, active being." The activity of spirits consists of both understanding and willing: understanding is spirit perceiving ideas, and will is spirit producing ideas.

For Berkeley, ostensibly physical objects like tables and chairs are really nothing more than collections of sensible ideas. Because no idea can exist outside a mind, it follows that tables and chairs, as well all the other furniture of the physical world, exist only insofar as they are in the mind of someone (i.e., only insofar as they are perceived). For any nonthinking being, *esse est percipi* ("to be is to be perceived").

The clichéd question of whether a tree falling in an uninhabited forest makes a sound is inspired by Berkeley's philosophy, though he never considered it in these terms.

Everyday objects such as tables and chairs might seem like physical things, but George Berkeley argued that they are only ideas. Shutterstock.com

He did, however, consider the implicit objection and gave various answers to it. He sometimes says that a table in an unperceived room would be perceived if someone were there. This conditional response, however, is inadequate. Granted that the table would exist if it were perceived, does it exist when it is not perceived? Berkeley's more pertinent answer is that, when no human is perceiving a table or other such object, God is; and it is God's thinking that keeps the otherwise unperceived object in existence.

Although this doctrine initially strikes most people as strange, Berkeley claimed that he was merely describing the commonsense view of reality. To say that colours, sounds, trees, dogs, and tables are ideas is not to say that they do not really exist, it is merely to say what they really are. Moreover, to say that animals and pieces of furniture are ideas is not to say that they are diaphanous, gossamer, and evanescent. Opacity, density, and permanence are also ideas that partially constitute these objects.

Berkeley supports his main thesis with a syllogistic argument: physical things such as trees, dogs, and houses are things perceived by sense; things perceived by sense are ideas; therefore, physical things are ideas. If one objects that the second premise of the syllogism is false—people sense things, not ideas—Berkeley would reply that there are no sensations without ideas and that it makes no sense to speak of some additional thing that ideas are supposed to represent or resemble. Unlike Locke, Berkeley did not believe that there is anything "behind" or "underlying" ideas in a world external to the mind. Indeed, Berkeley claims that no clear idea can be attached to this notion.

One consequence of this view is that Locke's distinction between primary and secondary qualities is spurious. Extension, figure, motion, rest, and solidity are as much ideas as green, loud, and bitter are; there is nothing special about the former kind of idea. Furthermore, matter, as philosophers conceive it, does not exist, and indeed it is contradictory. Although matter is supposedly unsensed extension, figure, and motion, because extension, figure, and motion are ideas, they must be sensed.

Berkeley's doctrine that things unperceived by human beings continue to exist in the thought of God was not novel. It was part of the traditional belief of Christian philosophers from Augustine through Aquinas and at least to Descartes that God not only creates all things but also keeps them in existence by thinking of them. According to this view, if God were ever to stop thinking of a creature, it would immediately be annihilated.

DAVID HUME

The third, and in many ways the most important, of the British empiricists was the skeptic David Hume. Hume's philosophical intention was to reap, humanistically, the harvest sowed by Newtonian physics, to apply the method of natural science to human nature. The paradoxical result of this admirable goal, however, was a devastating skeptical crisis.

KINDS OF PERCEPTION

Although Berkeley rejected the Lockean notions of primary and secondary qualities and matter, he retained Locke's beliefs in the existence of mind, substance, and causation as an unseen force or power in objects. Hume, in contrast, rejected all these notions.

Hume recognized two kinds of perception: *impressions* and *ideas*. Impressions are perceptions that the mind experiences with the "most force and violence," and ideas are the "faint images" of impressions. Hume considered this distinction so obvious that he demurred from explaining it at any length: as he indicates in a summary explication in *A Treatise of Human Nature*, impressions are felt, and ideas are thought. Nevertheless, he concedes that sometimes sleep, fever, or madness can produce ideas that approximate to the force of impressions, and some impressions can approach the weakness of ideas. But such occasions are rare.

The distinction between impressions and ideas is problematic in a way that Hume did not notice. The impression (experience) of anger, for example, has an unmistakable quality and intensity. But the idea of anger is not the same as a "weaker" experience of anger. Thinking of anger no more guarantees being angry than thinking of happiness guarantees being happy. So there seems to be a

David Hume, oil painting by Allan Ramsay, 1766, in the Scottish National Portrait Gallery, Edinburgh. Courtesy of the Scottish National Portrait Gallery

difference between the impression of anger and the idea of anger that Hume's theory does not capture.

All perceptions, whether impressions or ideas, can be either simple or complex. Although simple perceptions are not subject to further separation or distinction, complex perceptions are. To return to an example mentioned earlier, the perception of an apple is complex, insofar as it consists of a combination of simple perceptions of a certain shape, colour, texture, and aroma. It is noteworthy that, according to Hume, for every simple impression there is a simple idea that corresponds to it and differs from it only in force and vivacity, and vice versa. Thus, corresponding to the impression of red is the idea of red. This correlation does not hold true in general for complex perceptions. Although there is a correspondence between the complex impression of an apple and the complex idea of an apple, there is no impression that corresponds to the idea of Pegasus or the idea of a unicorn. These complex ideas do not have a correlate in reality. Similarly, there is no complex idea corresponding to the complex impression of, say, an extensive vista of the city of Rome.

Because the formation of every simple idea is always preceded by the experience of a corresponding simple impression, and because the experience of every simple impression is always followed by the formation of a corresponding simple idea, it follows, according to Hume, that simple impressions are the causes of their corresponding simple ideas.

There are two kinds of impressions: those of sensation and those of reflection. Regarding the former, Hume says little more than that sensation "arises in the soul originally from unknown causes." Impressions of reflection arise from a complicated series of mental operations. First, one experiences impressions of heat or cold, thirst or hunger, pleasure or pain. Second, one forms corresponding ideas of heat or cold, thirst or hunger, pleasure or pain. And third, one's reflection on these ideas produces impressions of "desire and aversion, hope and fear."

Because the faculty of imagination can divide and assemble disparate ideas at will, some explanation is needed for the fact that people tend to think in regular and predictable patterns. Hume says that the production of thoughts in the mind is guided by three principles: resemblance, contiguity, and cause and effect. Thus, a person who thinks of one idea is likely to think of another idea that resembles it. His thought is likely to run from red to pink to white or from dog to wolf to coyote. Concerning contiguity, people are inclined to think of things that are next to each other in space and time. Finally and most importantly, people tend to create associations between ideas of things that are causally related. The ideas of fire and smoke, parent and child, and disease and death are connected in the mind for this reason.

Hume uses the principle of resemblance for another purpose: to explain the nature of general ideas. Holding that there are no abstract ideas, Hume affirms that all ideas are particular. Some of them, however, function as general ideas (i.e., ideas that represent many objects of a certain kind) because they incline the mind to think of other ideas that they resemble.

RELATIONS OF IDEAS AND MATTERS OF FACT

According to Hume, the mind is capable of apprehending two kinds of proposition or truth: those expressing "relations of ideas" and those expressing "matters of fact." The former can be intuited (i.e., apprehended directly) or deduced from other propositions. That a is identical with a, that b resembles c, and that d is larger than e are examples of propositions that are intuited. The negations of true propositions expressing relations of ideas are contradictory.

Because the propositions of arithmetic and algebra are exclusively about relations of ideas, these disciplines are more certain than others. In the *Treatise*, Hume says that geometry is not quite as certain as arithmetic and algebra, because its original principles derive from sensation, and about sensation there can never be absolute certainty. He revised his views later, however, and in the *An Enquiry Concerning Human Understanding* (1748) he put geometry on an equal footing with the other mathematical sciences.

Unlike propositions about relations of ideas, propositions about matters of fact are known only through experience. By far the most important of these propositions are those that express or presuppose causal relations (e.g., "Fire causes heat" and "A moving billiard ball communicates its motion to any stationary ball it strikes"). But how is it possible to know through experience that one kind of object or event causes another? What kind of experience would justify such a claim?

CAUSE AND EFFECT

In the *Treatise*, Hume observes that the idea of causation contains three components: contiguity (i.e., near proximity) of time and place, temporal priority of the cause, and a more mysterious component that he calls "necessary connection." In other words, when one says that x is a cause of y, one means that instances of x and instances of y are always near each other in time and space, instances of x occur before instances of y, and there is some connection between x's and y's that makes it necessary that an instance of y occurs if an instance of x does.

It is easy to explain the origin in experience of the first two components of the idea of causation. In past experience, all events consisting of a moving billiard ball striking a stationary one were quickly followed by events consisting of the movement of the formerly stationary ball. In addition, the first sort of event always preceded the second, and never the reverse. But whence the third component of the idea of causation, whereby one thinks that the striking of the stationary ball somehow necessitates that it will move? Unlike the contiguity and temporal order of the striking and moving of billiard balls, no one has seen or otherwise directly observed this necessity in past experience.

It is important to note that, were it not for the idea of necessary connection, one would have no reason to believe that a currently observed cause will produce an unseen effect in the future or that a currently observed effect was produced by an unseen cause in the past. For the mere fact that past instances of the cause and effect were contiguous and temporally ordered in a certain way does not logically imply that present and future instances will display the same relations. (Such an inference could be justified only if one assumed a principle such as "*instances, of which we have had no experience, must resemble those, of which we have had experience, and that the course of nature continues always uniformly the same.*" The problem with this principle is that it too stands in need of justification, and the only possible justification is question-begging. That is, one could argue that present and future experience will resemble past experience, because, in the past, present and future experience resembled past experience. But this argument clearly assumes what it sets out to prove.)

Hume offers a "skeptical solution" of the problem of the origin of the idea of necessary connection. According to him, it arises from the feeling of "determination" that is created in the mind when it experiences the first member of a pair of events that it is long accustomed to experiencing together. When the mind observes the moving billiard ball strike the stationary one, it is moved by force of habit and custom to form an idea of the movement of the stationary ball (i.e., to believe that the stationary ball will move). The feeling of being "carried along" in this process is the impression from which the idea of necessary connection is derived. Hume's solution is "skeptical" in the sense that, though it accounts for the origins of the idea of necessary connection, it does not make causal inferences any more rational than they were before. The solution explains why people are psychologically compelled to form beliefs about future effects and past causes, but it does not justify those beliefs logically. It remains true that the only evidence for such beliefs is past experience of contiguity and temporal precedence. "All inferences from experience, therefore, are effects of custom, not of reasoning." Thus, it is that custom, not reason, is the great guide of life.

SUBSTANCE

From the time of Plato, one of the most basic notions in philosophy has been *substance*—that whose existence does not depend upon anything else. For Locke, the substance of an object is the hidden *substratum* in which the object's properties inhere and on which they depend for their existence. One of the reasons for Hume's importance in the history of philosophy is that he rejected this notion. In keeping with his strict empiricism, he held that the idea of substance, if it answers to anything genuine, must arise from experience. But what kind of experience can this be? By its proponents' own definition, substance is that which underlies an object's properties, including its sensible properties. It is therefore in principle unobservable. Hume concludes, "We have therefore no idea of substance, distinct from that of a collection of particular qualities, nor have we any other meaning when we either talk or reason concerning it."

Furthermore, the things that earlier philosophers had assumed were substances are in fact "nothing but a collection of simple ideas, that are united by the imagination, and have a particular name assigned to them." Gold, to take Hume's example, is nothing but the collection of the ideas of yellow, malleable, fusible, and so on. Even the mind, or the "self," is only a "heap or collection of different perceptions united together by certain relations and suppos'd tho' falsely, to be endow'd with a perfect simplicity or identity."

This conclusion had important consequences for the problem of personal identity, to which Locke had devoted considerable attention. For if there is nothing to the mind but a collection of perceptions, there is no self that persists as the subject of these perceptions. Therefore, it does not make sense to speak of the subject of certain perceptions yesterday as the "same self," or the "same person," as the subject of certain perceptions today or in the future. There is no self or person there.

NONEPISTEMOLOGICAL MOVEMENTS

Although the school of British empiricism represented the mainstream of Enlightenment philosophy until the time of Kant, it was by no means the only type of philosophy that the 18th century produced. The Enlightenment, which was based on a few great fundamental ideas (such as the dedication to reason, the belief in moral and intellectual progress, the confidence in nature as a source of inspiration and value, and the search for tolerance and freedom in political and social institutions), generated many crosscurrents of intellectual and philosophical expression.

MATERIALISM AND SCIENTIFIC DISCOVERY

The profound influence of Locke spread to France, where it not only resulted in the skeptical empiricism of Voltaire but also united with mechanistic aspects of Cartesianism to produce an entire school of sensationalistic materialism, a combination of materialism and a form of empiricism according to which sense perception is the only kind of experience from which genuine knowledge derives. This position even found its way into many of the articles of the great French *Encyclopédie*, edited by Denis Diderot (1713–84) and Jean d'Alembert (1717–83), which was almost a complete compendium of the scientific and humanistic accomplishments of the 18th century.

Although the terms Middle Ages and Renaissance were not invented until well after the historical periods they designate, scholars of the 18th century called their age "the Enlightenment" with self-conscious enthusiasm and pride. It was an age of optimism and expectations of new beginnings. Great strides were made in chemistry and biological science. Jean-Baptiste de Monet, chevalier de Lamarck (1744–1829), Georges, Baron Cuvier (1769–1832), and Georges-Louis Leclerc, comte de Buffon (1707–88), introduced a new system of animal classification. In the eight years between 1766 and 1774, the chemical elements hydrogen, nitrogen, and oxygen were discovered. Foundations were being laid in psychology and the social sciences and in ethics and aesthetics. The work of Anne-Robert-Jacques Turgot, baron de L'Aulne (1727–81), and Montesquieu in France, Giambattista Vico (1668–1744) in Italy, and Adam Smith (1723–90) in Scotland marked the beginning of economics, politics, history, sociology, and jurisprudence as sciences. Hume, Bentham, and the British "moral sense" theorists were turning ethics into a specialized field of philosophical inquiry. And Anthony Ashley, 3rd earl of Shaftesbury (1671–1713), Edmund Burke (1729–97), Johann Gottsched (1700–66), and Alexander Baumgarten (1714–62) were laying the foundations for a systematic aesthetics, the philosophical study of beauty and taste.

SOCIAL AND POLITICAL PHILOSOPHY

Apart from epistemology, the most significant philosophical contributions of the Enlightenment were made in the fields of social and political philosophy. The *Two Treatises of Civil Government* (1690) by Locke and *The Social Contract* (1762) by Rousseau proposed justifications of political association grounded in the newer political requirements of the age. The Renaissance political philosophies of Machiavelli, Bodin, and Hobbes had presupposed or defended the absolute power of kings and rulers. But the Enlightenment theories of Locke and Rousseau championed the freedom and equality of citizens. It was a natural historical transformation. The 16th and 17th centuries were the age of absolutism; the chief problem of politics was that of maintaining internal order, and political theory was conducted in the language of national sovereignty. But the 18th century was the age of the democratic revolutions; the chief political problem was that of securing freedom and revolting against injustice, and political theory was expressed in the idiom of natural and inalienable rights.

JOHN LOCKE

Locke's political philosophy explicitly denied the divine right of kings and the absolute power of the sovereign. Instead, he insisted on a natural and universal right to freedom and equality. The state of nature in which human beings originally lived was not, as Hobbes imagined, intolerable, but it did have certain inconveniences. Therefore, people banded together to form society—as Aristotle taught, "not simply to live, but to live well." Political power, Locke argued, can never be exercised apart from its ultimate purpose, which is the common good, for the political contract is undertaken in order to preserve life, liberty, and property.

It follows from Locke's view that that there can be no subjection to power without consent, a fundamental principle of political liberalism (the doctrine according to which the central problem of politics is the protection and enhancement of individual freedom). Once political society has been founded, however, citizens are obligated to accept the decisions of a majority of their number. Such decisions are made on behalf of the majority by the legislature, but the ultimate power of choosing the legislature rests with the people. Even the powers of the legislature are not absolute, because the law of nature remains as a permanent standard and as a principle of protection against arbitrary authority.

Locke's importance as a political philosopher lies in the argument of the second treatise. He begins by defining political power as a

> right of making Laws with Penalties of Death, and consequently all less Penalties, for the Regulating and Preserving of Property, and of employing the force of the Community, in the Execution of such Laws and in defence of the Common-wealth from Foreign Injury, and all this only for the Publick Good.

Much of the remainder of the *Treatise* is a commentary on this paragraph.

John Locke's political thought was grounded in the notion of a social contract and in the importance of toleration, particularly concerning religion. Hulton Archive/Getty Images

The State of Nature and the Social Contract

Locke's definition of political power has an immediate moral dimension. It is a "right" of making laws and enforcing them for "the public good." Power for Locke never simply means "capacity" but always "morally sanctioned capacity." Morality pervades the whole arrangement of society, and it is this fact, tautologically, that makes society legitimate.

Locke's account of political society is based on a hypothetical consideration of the human condition before the beginning of communal life. In this "state of nature," humans are entirely free. But this freedom is not a state of complete license, because it is set within the bounds of the law of nature. It is a state of equality, which is itself a central element of Locke's account. In marked contrast to Filmer's world, there is no natural hierarchy among humans. Each person is naturally free and equal under the law of nature, subject only to the will of "the infinitely wise Maker." Each person, moreover, is required to enforce as well as to obey this law. It is this duty that gives to humans the right to punish offenders. But in such a state of nature, it is obvious that placing the right to punish in each person's hands may lead to injustice and violence. This can be remedied if humans enter into a contract with each other to recognize by common consent a civil government with the power to enforce the law of nature among the citizens of that state. Although any contract is legitimate as long as it does not infringe upon the law of nature, it often happens that a contract can be enforced only if there is some higher human authority to require compliance with it. It is a primary function of society to set up the framework in which legitimate contracts, freely entered into, may be enforced, a state of affairs much more difficult to guarantee in the state of nature and outside civil society.

Property

Before discussing the creation of political society in greater detail, Locke provides a lengthy account of his notion of property, which is of central importance to his political theory. Each person, according to Locke, has property in his own person—that is, each person literally owns his own body. Other people may not use a person's body for any purpose without his permission. But one can acquire property beyond one's own body through labour. By mixing one's labour with objects in the world, one acquires a right to the fruits of that work. If one's labour turns a barren field into crops or a pile of wood into a house, then the valuable product of that labour, the crops

According to John Locke, if one sows crops from a previously barren field, the products of that labor are one's property. Wallace Kirkland/Time & Life Pictures/Getty Images

or the house, becomes one's property. Locke's view was a forerunner of the labour theory of value, which was expounded in different forms by the 19th-century economists David Ricardo (1772–1823) and Karl Marx (1818–83).

Clearly, each person is entitled to as much of the product of his labour as he needs to survive. But, according to Locke, in the state of nature one is not entitled to hoard surplus produce. One must share it with those less fortunate. God has "given the World to Men in common . . . to make use of to the best advantage of Life, and convenience." The introduction of money, while radically changing the economic base of society, was itself a contingent development, for money has no intrinsic value but depends for its utility only on convention.

Locke's account of property and how it comes to be owned faces difficult problems. For example, it is far from clear how much labour is required to turn any given unowned object into a piece of private property. In the case of a piece of land, for example, is it sufficient merely to put a fence around it? Or must it be plowed as well? There is, nevertheless, something intuitively powerful in the notion that it is activity, or work, that grants one a property right in something.

Organization of Government

Locke returns to political society in Chapter VIII of the second treatise. In the community created by the social contract, the will of the majority should prevail, subject to the law of nature. The legislative body is central, but it cannot create laws that violate the law of nature, because the enforcement of the natural law regarding life, liberty, and property is the rationale of the whole system. Laws must apply equitably to all citizens and not favour particular sectional interests, and there should be a division of legislative, executive, and judicial powers. The legislature may, with the agreement of the majority, impose such taxes as are required to fulfill the ends of the state (including, of course, its defense). If the executive power fails to provide the conditions under which the people can enjoy their rights under natural law, the people are entitled to remove him, by force if necessary. Thus, revolution, in extremis, is permissible. Locke obviously thought so in 1688–89, when the Glorious Revolution resulted in the deposition of the English king, James II.

The significance of Locke's vision of political society can scarcely be exaggerated. His integration of individualism within the framework of the law of nature and his account of the origins and limits of legitimate government authority inspired the U.S. Declaration of Independence (1776) and the broad outlines of the system of government adopted in the U.S. Constitution. George Washington (1732–99), the first president of the United States, once described Locke as "the greatest man who had ever lived." In France too, Lockean principles found clear expression in the Declaration of the Rights of Man and of the Citizen (1789) and other justifications of the French Revolution.

JEAN-JACQUES ROUSSEAU

Rousseau's more radical political doctrines, as developed in his *Discours sur l'origine de l'inegalité* (1755; *Discourse on the Origin of Inequality*) and *Du Contrat social* (1762; *The Social Contract*), were built upon Lockean foundations. For him, too, the convention of the social contract formed the basis of all legitimate political authority, but his conception of citizenship was much more organic and much less individualistic than Locke's. The surrender of natural liberty for civil liberty means that all individual rights (among them property rights) become subordinate to the general will. For Rousseau the state is a moral person whose life is the union of its members, whose laws are acts of the

Rousseau, drawing in pastels by Maurice-Quentin de La Tour, 1753, from the Musée d'Art et d'Histoire, Geneva. Courtesy of the Musée d'Art et d'Histoire, Geneva; photograph, Jean Arlaud

general will, and whose end is the liberty and equality of its citizens. It follows that when any government usurps the power of the people, the social contract is broken. And not only are the citizens no longer compelled to obey, but they also have an obligation to rebel. Rousseau's defiant collectivism was clearly a revolt against Locke's systematic individualism; for Rousseau the fundamental category was not "natural person" but "citizen."

Discourse on the Origin of Inequality

Rousseau's *Discourse on the Origin of Inequality* was written in response to a question set by the Academy of Dijon: "What is the origin of the inequality among men and is it justified by natural law?" His answer was a masterpiece of speculative anthropology. The argument follows on that of an earlier work, the *Discours sur les sciences et les arts* (1750; *Discourse on the Sciences and the Arts*), by developing the proposition that humanity is naturally good and then tracing the successive stages by which humans have descended from primitive innocence to corrupt sophistication.

Rousseau begins by distinguishing two kinds of inequality, natural and artificial, the first arising from differences in strength, intelligence, and so forth, the second from the conventions that govern societies. He sets out to explain the inequalities of the latter sort. Adopting what he thought the properly "scientific" method of investigating origins, he attempts to reconstruct the earliest phases of human experience of life on Earth. He suggests that the first humans were not social beings but entirely solitary, and to this extent he agrees with Hobbes's account of the state of nature. But in contrast to the English pessimist's view that the life of people in such a condition must have been "poor, nasty, brutish and short," Rousseau claims that the first humans, while admittedly solitary, were healthy, happy, good, and free. Human vice, he argues, dates from the time when societies were formed.

Rousseau thus exonerates nature and blames society for the emergence of vices. He says that passions that generate vices hardly exist in the state of nature but begin to develop as soon as societies are formed. Rousseau goes on to suggest that societies started with the building of the first huts, a development that facilitated cohabitation of males and females, which in turn produced the habit of living as a family and associating with neighbours. This "nascent society," as Rousseau calls it, was good while it lasted. Indeed it was the "golden age" of human history. Only it did not endure. With the tender passion of love there was also born the destructive passion of jealousy. Neighbours started to compare their abilities and achievements with one another, and this "marked the first step towards inequality and at the same time towards vice." People started to demand consideration and respect. Their innocent self-love turned into culpable pride, as each person wanted to be better than everyone else.

The introduction of property marked a further step toward inequality because it made it necessary to institute law and government to protect property. Rousseau laments the "fatal" concept of property in one of his more eloquent passages, describing the "horrors" that have resulted from humanity's departure from a condition in which the Earth belonged to no one. These passages in his second *Discourse* excited later revolutionaries such as Marx and Vladimir Ilich Lenin (1870–1924), but Rousseau did not think that the past could be undone in any way. There was no point in dreaming of a return to the golden age.

Civil society, as Rousseau describes it, comes into being to serve two purposes: provide peace for everyone and ensure the right to property for anyone lucky enough to have possessions. It is thus of some advantage to everyone, but mostly to the advantage of the rich, because it transforms their de facto ownership into rightful ownership and keeps the poor dispossessed. It is a somewhat fraudulent social contract that introduces government because the poor get so much less out of it than do the rich. Even so, the rich are no happier in civil society than are the poor because in society people are never satisfied. Society leads people to hate one another to the extent that their interests conflict, and at best they are able to hide their hostility behind a mask of courtesy. Thus Rousseau regards inequality not as a separate problem but as one of the features of the long process by which people became alienated from nature and from innocence.

The Social Contract

Like Plato, Rousseau always believed that a just society was one in which everyone was in his right place. And having written the *Discourse* to explain how people had lost their liberty in the past, he went on to write another book, *The Social Contract*, to suggest how they might recover their liberty in the future.

The Social Contract begins with the sensational sentence, "Man is born free, and everywhere he is in chains," and proceeds to argue that he need not be in chains. If a civil society, or state, could be based on a genuine social contract, as opposed to the fraudulent social contract depicted in the *Discourse on the Origin of Inequality*, people would receive in exchange for their independence a better kind of freedom, namely true political, or republican, liberty. Such liberty is to be found in obedience to a self-imposed law.

Rousseau's definition of political liberty raises an obvious problem. For while it can be readily agreed that an individual is free if he obeys only rules he prescribes for himself. This is so because an individual is a person with a single will. A society, by contrast, is a set of persons with a set of individual wills, and conflict between separate wills is a fact of universal experience. Rousseau's response to the problem is to define his civil society as an artificial person united by a *volonté générale,* or "general will." The social contract that brings society into being is a pledge, and the society remains in being as a pledged group. Rousseau's republic is a creation of the general will—of a will that never falters in each and every member to further the public, common, or national interest—even though it may conflict at times with personal interest.

Rousseau sounds much like Hobbes when he says that under the pact by which individuals enter civil society each person totally alienates himself and all his rights to the whole community. Rousseau, however, represents this act as a form of exchange of rights whereby individuals give up natural rights in return for civil rights. The bargain is a good one because what is surrendered are rights of dubious value, whose realization depends solely on an individual's own might, and what is obtained in return are rights that are both legitimate and enforced by the collective force of the community.

There is no more haunting paragraph in *The Social Contract* than that in which Rousseau speaks of "forcing a man to be free." But it would be wrong to interpret these words in the manner of those critics who see Rousseau as a prophet of modern totalitarianism. He does not claim that a whole society can be forced to be free but only that an occasional individual, who is enslaved by his passions to the extent of disobeying the law, can be restored by force to obedience to the voice of the general will that exists inside of him. The person who is coerced by society for a breach of the law is, in Rousseau's view, being brought back to an awareness of his own true interests.

For Rousseau there is a radical dichotomy between true law and actual law. Actual law, which he describes in the *Discourse on the Origin of Inequality,* simply protects the status quo. True law, as described in *The Social Contract,* is just law, and what ensures its being just is that it is made by the people in its collective capacity as sovereign and obeyed by the same people in their individual capacities as subjects. Rousseau is confident that such laws could not be unjust because it is inconceivable that any people would make unjust laws for itself.

Rousseau is, however, troubled by the fact that the majority of a people does not necessarily represent its most intelligent citizens. Indeed, he agrees with Plato that most people are stupid. Thus the general will, while always morally sound, is sometimes mistaken. Hence Rousseau suggests the people need a lawgiver—a great mind like the Athenian statesmen Solon (*c.* 630–*c.* 560 BCE) and Lycurgus (*c.* 390–*c.* 324 BCE) or the Reformer John Calvin (1509–64)—to draw up a constitution and system of laws. He even suggests that such lawgivers need to claim divine inspiration to persuade the dim-witted multitude to accept and endorse the laws it is offered.

This suggestion echoes a similar proposal by Machiavelli, whom Rousseau greatly admired and whose love of republican government he shared. An even more conspicuously Machiavellian influence can be discerned in Rousseau's chapter on civil religion, where he argues that Christianity, despite its truth, is useless as a republican religion on the grounds that it is directed to the unseen world and does nothing to teach citizens the virtues that are needed in the service of the state: namely, courage, virility, and patriotism. Rousseau does not go so far as Machiavelli in proposing a revival of pagan cults, but he does propose a civil religion with minimal theological content designed to fortify and not impede (as Christianity impedes) the cultivation of martial virtues.

IMMANUEL KANT

The epistemological theories of the British empiricists led directly to the philosophy of Immanuel Kant, the most important philosopher of the modern period, whose works mark the true culmination of the philosophy of the Enlightenment. Kant acknowledged that Hume had awakened him from a "dogmatic slumber." Although Kant's subsequent "critical" philosophy emphasized the limitations of human reason, it did so in a manner that ultimately vindicated the claims to knowledge that more traditional philosophers had made on its behalf.

The problem of knowledge, according to Kant, is to explain how some judgments about the world can be necessarily true and therefore knowable a priori, or independently of experience. Until Kant's time, all empirical judgments were regarded as vulnerable to skeptical doubt, because human experience is inherently fallible. Furthermore, all a priori judgments, such as "All bachelors are unmarried," were regarded as empty of content, because they did not present any information that was not already contained in the concepts with which they were composed (being unmarried is part of what it is to be a bachelor). If human knowledge of the world was to be possible, therefore, there would have to be judgments that were both empirical and a priori.

The genius and originality of Kant's philosophy lay in the means by which he made room for such judgments. In what he described, in the preface to the second edition (1787) of the *Kritik der reinen Vernunft* (*Critique of Pure Reason*), as his "Copernican" revolution, he proposed that knowledge should not depend on the conformity of a

Immanuel Kant, print published in London, 1812. Photos.com/ Jupiterimages

judgment to an object in experience. Rather, the existence of an object in experience should depend on its conformity to human knowledge.

> *Hitherto it has been assumed that all our knowledge must conform to objects. But all attempts to extend our knowledge of objects by establishing something in regard to them a priori, by means of concepts, have, on this assumption, ended in failure. We must therefore make trial whether we may not have more success in the tasks of metaphysics, if we suppose that objects must conform to our knowledge.*

That is to say, a thing can be an "object of possible experience" for human beings only if it conforms to human knowledge in certain respects. This is because the faculty of intuition—which receives the appearances ("phenomena") of experience—is structured by the concepts of space and time, and because the faculty of understanding—which orders the phenomena received through intuition—is structured by concepts grouped under the general headings of quantity, quality, relation, and modality. The fact that space and time are forms of possible experience, rather than generalizations derived from experience, explains how the judgments of geometry, for example, can be both empirical (about experience) and knowable a priori. Similarly, a judgment such as "Every event has a cause," is both empirical and a priori, because causality (under the heading "relation") is one of the concepts imposed on experience by the understanding, not a generalization derived by the understanding from experience.

Behind the phenomena of experience, according to Kant, there is a realm of "noumena" (e.g., "things in themselves") that is in principle unknowable. Traditional philosophers mistakenly assumed that reason could use a priori principles to derive metaphysical knowledge of things outside or beyond any possible experience. In this respect the skeptical philosophers had been right to criticize the traditional proofs of the existence of God or of the immortality of the soul as so much empty dogmatism.

Not surprisingly, neither of Kant's chief philosophical antagonists was satisfied with the new critical philosophy. For the skeptics, Kant's distinction between phenomena and noumena was redolent of earlier metaphysics. If knowledge of the noumenal realm is impossible, on what basis could Kant claim that it exists? Why refer to it at all? For the dogmatists, however, Kant's supposed defense of the powers of reason ceded far too much ground to the antimetaphysical camp.

Kant's moral philosophy, as elaborated in the *Kritik der practischen Vernunft* (1788; *Critique of Practical Reason*) and the *Grundlegung zur Metaphysik der Sitten* (1785; *Groundwork of the Metaphysics of Morals*), also proved extremely influential. In these works his central concern was human freedom, or the autonomy of the will, just as the autonomy of reason had been the focus of the first critique. The immediate problem for Kant was to reconcile the idea of freedom with the evident causal determinism operative in the phenomenal world, a determinism that the first critique itself had endorsed.

Against the champions of determinism, Kant insisted on the autonomous capacities of the human will: by universalizing one's maxims (or reasons) for action in accordance with the categorical imperative, "Act only according to that maxim by which you can at the same time will that it should become a universal law," one acts freely, or autonomously. By following universal imperatives, the will escapes the contingencies and determinism of the phenomenal or empirical realm. Thereby, its actions obtain an ethical dignity or moral purity that approximates the sublimity of what Kant called the "kingdom of ends": a noumenal realm of pure morality, unaffected by the vagaries of experience. In Kant's ethical theory, the kingdom of ends possesses the sublimity of an idea of pure reason, inasmuch as it is free of empirical taint. Kant's formula for autonomy is thus opposed to utilitarianism, the view that actions are right or wrong by virtue of their consequences. Whereas utilitarian moral theories suggest that morally right actions are properly motivated by desires or interests (e.g., to maximize consequences that are good, such as pleasure or happiness) Kant's brand of moral rigorism is predicated on reason alone.

Yet, Kant openly admitted that, according to the letter of his approach, human freedom possesses a merely "formal" or "noumenal" character. Once one tries to act freely in a phenomenal world dominated by the principle of causality, or to act morally in a world in which human action is always motivated by interests, "rational" or "free" outcomes cannot be guaranteed. Thus, Kant's practical philosophy is beset by the antinomy (contradiction) between freedom and necessity: human beings are inwardly free but outwardly subject to the laws of causality. This Pyrrhic vindication of freedom left many of Kant's heirs dissatisfied and striving vigorously to transcend the oppositions and limitations his philosophy had bequeathed.

CHAPTER 4

THE 19TH CENTURY

K ant's death in 1804 formally marked the end of the Enlightenment. The 19th century ushered in new philosophical problems and new conceptions of what philosophy ought to do. It was a century of great philosophical diversity. In the Renaissance, the chief intellectual fact had been the rise of mathematics and natural science, and the tasks that this fact imposed upon philosophy determined its direction for two centuries. In the Enlightenment, attention had turned to the character of the mind that had so successfully mastered the natural world, and rationalists and empiricists had contended for mastery until the Kantian synthesis. As for the 19th century, however, if one single feature of its thought could be singled out for emphasis, it might be called the discovery of the irrational. But many philosophical schools were present, and they contended with each other in a series of distinct and powerful oppositions: pragmatism against idealism, positivism against irrationalism, Marxism against liberalism.

Western philosophy in the 19th century was influenced by several changes in European and American intellectual culture and society. These changes were chiefly the Romantic Movement of the early 19th century, which was a poetic revolt against reason in favour of feeling; the maturation of the Industrial

Revolution, which caused untold misery as well as prosperity and prompted a multitude of philosophies of social reform; the revolutions of 1848 in Paris, Germany, and Vienna, which reflected stark class divisions and first implanted in the European consciousness the concepts of the bourgeoisie and the proletariat; and, finally, the great surge in biological science following the publication of work by Charles Darwin (1809–82) on the theory of evolution. Romanticism influenced both German idealists and philosophers of irrationalism. Experiences of economic discord and social unrest produced the ameliorative social philosophy of English utilitarianism and the revolutionary doctrines of Karl Marx. And the developmental ideas of Darwin provided the prerequisites for American pragmatism.

A synoptic view of Western philosophy in the 19th century reveals an interesting chronology. The early century was dominated by the German school of absolute idealism, whose main representatives were Johann Fichte (1762–1814), Friedrich Schelling (1775–1854), and Georg Wilhelm Friedrich Hegel (1770–1831). The mid-century was marked by a rebirth of interest in science and its methods, as reflected in the work of Auguste Comte (1798–1857) in France and John Stuart Mill (1806–73) in England, and by liberal (Mill) and radical (Marx) social theory. The late century experienced a second flowering of idealism, this time led by the English philosophers T.H. Green (1836–82), F.H. Bradley (1846–1924), and Bernard Bosanquet (1848–1923), and the rise of American pragmatism, represented by Charles Sanders Peirce (1839–1914) and William James (1842–1910). The new philosophies of the irrational, produced by the highly idiosyncratic thinkers Arthur Schopenhauer (1788–1860), Søren Kierkegaard (1813–55), and Friedrich Nietzsche (1844–1900), ran through the century in its entirety.

Søren Kierkegaard's emphasis on the desolate human condition and the uncertainty of salvation made him a major influence on existentialism and Protestant theology. Hulton Archive/Getty Images

GERMAN IDEALISM

The Enlightenment, inspired by the example of natural science, had accepted certain boundaries to human knowledge. That is, it had recognized certain limits to reason's ability to penetrate ultimate reality because that would require methods that surpass the capabilities of scientific method. In this particular modesty, the philosophies of Hume and Kant were much alike. But in the early 19th century, the metaphysical spirit returned in a most ambitious and extravagant form. German idealism reinstated the most speculative pretensions of Leibniz and Spinoza. This development resulted in part from the influence of Romanticism but also, and more importantly, from a new alliance of philosophy with religion. It was not a coincidence that all the great German idealists were either former students of theology (Fichte at Jena and Leipzig, Schelling and Hegel at the Tübingen seminary) or the sons of Protestant pastors. It is probably this circumstance that gave to German idealism its intensely serious, quasi-religious, and dedicated character.

The consequence of this religious alignment was that philosophical interest shifted from Kant's *Critique of Pure Reason* (in which he attempted to account for natural science and denied the possibility of certainty in metaphysics) to his *Critique of Practical Reason* (in which he explored the nature of the moral self) and his *Critique of Judgment* (in which he treated of the purposiveness of the universe as a whole). Absolute idealism was based on three premises:

1. The chief datum of philosophy is the human self and its self-consciousness.
2. The world as a whole is spiritual through and through (that it is, in fact, something like a cosmic self).

3. In both the self and the world, it is not primarily the intellectual element that counts but, rather, the volitional and the moral.

Thus, for idealistic metaphysics, the primary task of philosophy was understanding the self, self-consciousness, and the spiritual universe.

JOHANN GOTTLIEB FICHTE

Johann Gottlieb Fichte conceived of human self-consciousness as the primary metaphysical fact. Taking Kant's *Critique of Practical Reason* as his starting point, he held that, just as the moral will is the chief characteristic of the self, so it is also the activating principle of the world. According to Fichte, all being is posited by the ego, which posits itself. As he stated in *Das System der Sittenlehre nach den Prinzipien der Wissenschaftslehre* (1798; *The Science of Ethics as Based on the Science of Knowledge*), "That whose being (essence) consists merely in the fact that it posits itself as existent is the ego as absolute subject. As it posits itself, so it is; and as it is, so it posits itself." In Fichte's view, if the ego is in reality the basis of all experience, it qualifies as "unconditioned": it is free of empirical taint and no longer subject to the limitations of causality emanating from the external world. In this way, Kant's antithesis or opposition between the noumenal and phenomenal realms disappears.

Fichte gave a practical or voluntarist cast to the dictum *cogito, ergo sum*, which Descartes had proposed as the bedrock of certainty on which the edifice of human knowledge could be constructed. As the German writer Johann Wolfgang von Goethe (1749–1832) would remark, in a Fichtean spirit, in *Faust* (1808), "In the beginning was the deed." However, on the whole Fichte's heirs remained unsatisfied with his voluntaristic resolution of the tension between subject and object, will and experience. They perceived his claims as little more than an abstract declaration rather than a substantive resolution or authentic working through of the problem. Subsequent thinkers also wondered whether his elevation of the subject to the position of an absolute did not result in an impoverishment of experience.

GEORG WILHELM FRIEDRICH HEGEL

Kant's most important successor, Georg Wilhelm Friedrich Hegel, attempted to transcend systematically all the antinomies of Kantian thought: noumenon and phenomenon, freedom and necessity, subject and object. Kant had claimed that humans could aspire only to knowledge of phenomena, whereas Hegel set out to prove that, as in the metaphysics of old, reason was in fact capable of an "absolute knowledge" that penetrated into essences, or things-in-themselves. For Kant the ideas of pure reason possessed merely a noumenal status: they could serve as regulative ideals for human thought or achievement, yet, insofar as they transcended the bounds of experience, they could never be verified or redeemed by the understanding.

In Hegel's thought the limitations to knowledge repeatedly stressed by Kant had become nothing less than a scandal. As Hegel declared polemically in the *Wissenschaft der Logik* (1812, 1816; *Science of Logic*), "The Kantian philosophy becomes a pillow for intellectual sloth, which soothes itself with the idea that everything has been already proved and done with." Hegel's major works, including, in addition to the *Science of Logic*, the *Phänomenologie des Geistes* (1807; *Phenomenology of Spirit*) and the *Grundlinien der Philosophie des Rechts* (1821; Eng.

G.W.F. Hegel, oil painting by Jakob von Schlesinger, c. 1825, in the Staatliche Museum, Berlin. Deutsche Fotothek, Dresden

trans. *The Philosophy of Right*), all contain detailed and powerful rejoinders to Kantian conceptions of knowledge, truth, and freedom.

For Hegel the challenge was to articulate a philosophy that went beyond Kant without regressing behind him by relapsing into dogmatic metaphysics. In the *Phenomenology of Spirit*, Hegel undertook a genuinely novel approach to the problem of knowledge, tracing the immanent movement of the "shapes of consciousness" (the different historical conceptions of knowledge) from "sense certainty" through "perception," "force," "consciousness," "self-consciousness," "reason," "spirit," and finally "absolute knowing." At the final stage, "otherness" has been eliminated, and consciousness has reached the plane of unconditional truth. At this point a conception of knowledge is obtained (which Hegel called the *Begriff*, or idea) that is free of the aforementioned Kantian oppositions and thus suitable for producing a "first philosophy": a doctrine of essences that accurately captures the rational structure of reality. No longer limited, as with Kant, to knowledge of appearances, consciousness is at last able to obtain genuine knowledge of the way things truly are.

Announcing his philosophical program in the *Phenomenology of Spirit*, Hegel declared that "substance must become subject." This terse formula characterized one of his main philosophical goals: to reconcile classical and modern philosophy. In Hegel's view, Greek philosophy had attained an adequate notion of substance yet for historical reasons had fallen short of the modern concept of subjectivity. Conversely, modern philosophy, beginning with Descartes, appreciated the value of subjectivity as a philosophical starting point but failed to develop an adequate notion of objective truth. Hegel's philosophy sought to combine the virtues of both approaches by linking ontology (the philosophical study of being, or existence) and epistemology (the philosophical study of knowledge).

At the same time, Hegel believed that by embracing subjectivity Kant and other modern philosophers had prematurely abandoned the claims of ontology. By making truth inordinately dependent on the standpoint of the knowing subject, they failed to give "essence," or the intrinsic nature of objective reality, its due. Consequently, their philosophies were tainted by "subjectivism." In Kant's case, this defect was evident in his conclusion that phenomena are the only possible objects of knowledge as well as in the solipsistic implications of his moral doctrine, which posited mutually isolated subjects who formulate universal laws valid for all moral agents. The Kantian moral subject, which prized autonomy above all else, radically devalued habit, custom, and tradition: what Hegel described as substantial ethical life, or *Sittlichkeit*. In Hegel's view, these modern approaches placed a burden on the idea of subjectivity that was more than the concept could bear. In this regard as well, Hegel sought a compromise between modernity's extreme devaluation of tradition and the elements of rootedness and continuity that it could provide, thereby preventing the autonomous subject from spinning out of control as it were.

Hegel thought that he discerned the disastrous consequences of such willfulness in the rise of bourgeois society—which he perceived, following Thomas Hobbes, as a competitive "war of all against all"—and in the despotic outcome of the French Revolution. Because bourgeois society, whose doctrine of "rights" had elevated the modern subject to a virtual absolute, gave unfettered rein to individual liberty, it invited anarchy, with tyranny as the only stopgap. Hegel held Kant's philosophy to be the consummate expression of this modern standpoint, with all its debilities and risks. Consequently, in his political philosophy Hegel argued that substantial ethical life resided in the state. In his view, the state alone was capable of reconciling the antagonisms and contradictions of bourgeois society. The quietistic (if not reactionary) implications of his political thought were epitomized by his famous declaration in *The Philosophy of Right* that "what is rational is actual, and what is actual is rational."

Moreover, it became increasingly difficult for Hegel's followers to defend his later philosophy against the charge of having regressed to a pre-Kantian metaphysical dogmatism. In the *Science of Logic*, Hegel presumptuously claimed that his treatise contained "the thoughts of God before He created the world." Later critics would strongly object to his "pan-logism": his a priori assumption that the categories of reason necessarily underlay the whole of reality, or being. Although Hegel optimistically proclaimed that history demonstrated "progress in the consciousness of freedom," his doctrine of the "cunning of reason"—according to which the aims of the World Spirit are willy-nilly realized behind the backs of individual actors—appeared to justify misery and injustice in the world as part of a larger plan visible only to Hegel himself. "History," he observed unapologetically, is "the slaughter-bench on which the happiness of peoples, the wisdom of states, and the virtue of individuals have been sacrificed."

SOCIAL AND POLITICAL THEORY

The absolute idealists wrote as if the Renaissance methodologists of the sciences had never existed. But if in Germany the empirical and scientific tradition in philosophy lay dormant, in France and England in the middle of the 19th century it was very much alive.

THE POSITIVISM OF AUGUSTE COMTE

In France, the philosopher and social theorist Auguste
Comte wrote his great philosophical history of science,
Cours de philosophie positive (1830–42; Eng. trans. *The
Positive Philosophy of Auguste Comte*), in six volumes.
Influenced by Francis Bacon and the entire school of
British empiricism, by the doctrine of progress put forward by the marquis de Condorcet (1743–94) and others
during the 18th century, and by the original social reformer
Henri de Saint-Simon (1760–1825), Comte called his philosophy "positivism," by which he meant a philosophy of
science so narrow that it denied any validity whatsoever to
"knowledge" not derived through the accepted methods
of science.

Comte lived through the aftermath of the French
Revolutionary and Napoleonic periods, at a time when a
new, stable social order—without despotism—was sought.
Modern science and technology and the Industrial
Revolution had begun transforming the societies of
Europe in directions no one yet understood. People experienced violent conflict but were adrift in feeling, thought,
and action. They lacked confidence in established senti-
ments, beliefs, and institutions but had nothing with
which to replace them. Comte thought that this condition was not only significant for France and Europe but
was one of the decisive junctures of human history.

Comte's particular ability was as a synthesizer of the
most diverse intellectual currents. He took his ideas
mainly from writers of the 18th and early 19th centuries.
From David Hume and Immanuel Kant he derived his
conception of positivism (i.e., the theory that theology
and metaphysics are earlier imperfect modes of knowledge and that positive knowledge is based on natural

phenomena and their properties and relations as verified by the empirical sciences). From various French clericalist thinkers Comte took the notion of a hypothetical frame-work for social organization that would imitate the hierarchy and discipline found in the Roman Catholic Church. From various Enlightenment philosophers he adopted the notion of historical progress. Most important, from Saint-Simon he came to appreciate the need for a basic and unifying social science that would both explain existing social organizations and guide social planning for a better future. This new science he called "sociology" for the first time.

Comte shared Saint-Simon's appreciation of the growing importance of modern science and the potential application of scientific methods to the study and improvement of society. Comte believed that social phenomena could be reduced to laws in the same way that the revolutions of the heavenly bodies had been made explicable by gravitational theory. Furthermore, he believed that the purpose of the new scientific analysis of society should be ameliorative and that the ultimate outcome of all innovation and systematization in the new science should be the guidance of social planning. Comte also thought a new and secularized spiritual order was needed to supplant what he viewed as the outdated supernaturalism of Christian theology.

Comte's main contribution to positivist philosophy falls into five parts: his rigorous adoption of the scientific method; his law of the three states or stages of intellectual development; his classification of the sciences; his conception of the incomplete philosophy of each of these sciences anterior to sociology; and his synthesis of a positivist social philosophy in a unified form. He sought a system of philosophy that could form a basis for political organization appropriate to modern industrial society.

Comte's "law of the three stages" maintained that human intellectual development had moved historically from a theological stage, in which the world and human destiny within it were explained in terms of gods and spirits; through a transitional metaphysical stage, in which explanations were in terms of essences, final causes, and other abstractions; and finally to the modern positive stage. This last stage was distinguished by an awareness of the limitations of human knowledge. Knowledge could only be relative to man's nature as a species and to his varying social and historical situations. Absolute explanations were therefore better abandoned for the more sensible discovery of laws based on the observable relations between phenomena.

Comte's classification of the sciences was based on the hypothesis that the sciences had developed from the understanding of simple and abstract principles to the understanding of complex and concrete phenomena. Hence, the sciences developed as follows: from mathematics, astronomy, physics, and chemistry to biology and finally to sociology. According to Comte, this last discipline not only concluded the series but would also reduce social facts to laws and synthesize the whole of human knowledge, thus rendering the discipline equipped to guide the reconstruction of society.

Although Comte did not originate the concept of sociology or its area of study, he greatly extended and elaborated the field and systematized its content. Comte divided sociology into two main fields, or branches: social statics, or the study of the forces that hold society together; and social dynamics, or the study of the causes of social change. He held that the underlying principles of society are individual egoism, which is encouraged by the division of labour, and the combination of efforts and the maintenance of social cohesion by means of government and the state.

Comte revealed his conception of the ideal positivist society in his *Système de politique positive*, 4 vol. (1851–54; *System of Positive Polity*). He believed that the organization of the Roman Catholic church, divorced from Christian theology, could provide a structural and symbolic model for the new society, though Comte substituted a "religion of humanity" for the worship of God. A spiritual priesthood of secular sociologists would guide society and control education and public morality. The actual administration of the government and of the economy would be in the hands of businessmen and bankers, and the maintenance of private morality would be the province of women as wives and mothers.

Although unquestionably a man of genius, Comte inspired discipleship on the one hand and derision on the other. His plans for a future society have been described as ludicrous, and Comte was deeply reactionary in his rejection of democracy, his emphasis on hierarchy and obedience, and his opinion that the ideal government would be made up of an intellectual elite. But his ideas influenced such notable social scientists as Émile Durkheim (1858–1917) of France and Herbert Spencer (1820–1903) and Sir Edward Burnett Tylor (1832–1917) of Britain. Comte's belief in the importance of sociology as the scientific study of human society remains an article of faith among contemporary sociologists, and the work he accomplished remains a remarkable synthesis and an important system of thought.

THE UTILITARIANISM OF JEREMY BENTHAM AND JOHN STUART MILL

A major force in the political and social thought of the 19th century was utilitarianism, the doctrine that the actions of governments, as well as individuals, should be judged simply by the extent to which they promoted the "greatest happiness of the greatest number." The founder of the utilitarian school was Jeremy Bentham (1748–1832), an English philosopher, economist, and theoretical jurist. Bentham judged all laws and institutions by their utility thus defined. "The Fabric of Felicity," he wrote, "must be reared by the hands of reason and Law."

Bentham's *Fragment, on Government* (1776) and *Introduction to the Principles of Morals and Legislation* (1789) elaborated a utilitarian political philosophy. Bentham was an atheist and an exponent of the new laissez-faire economics of Adam Smith and David Ricardo, but he inspired the spate of legislation that, after the Reform Bill of 1832, had tackled the worst consequences of 18th-century inefficiency and of the Industrial Revolution. His influence, moreover, spread widely abroad. At first a simple reformer of law, Bentham attacked notions of contract and natural law as superfluous. "The indestructible prerogatives of mankind," he wrote, "have no need to be supported upon the sandy foundation of a fiction." The justification of government is pragmatic, its aim improvement and the release of the free choice of individuals and the play of market forces that will create prosperity. Bentham thought society could advance by calculation of pleasure and pain, and his *Introduction* even tries to work out "the value of a lot of pleasure and pain, how now to be measured." He compared the relative gratifications of health, wealth, power, friendship, and benevolence, as well as those of "irascible appetite" and "antipathy." He also thought of punishment purely as a deterrent, not as retribution, and graded offenses on the harm they did to happiness, not on how much they offended God or tradition.

If Bentham's psychology was naïve, that of his disciple James Mill was philistine. Mill postulated an economic individual whose decisions, if freely taken, would always be in his own interest, and he believed that universal suffrage, along with utilitarian legislation by a sovereign parliament, would produce the kind of happiness and well-being that Bentham desired. In his *Essay on Government* (1828) Mill thus shows a doctrinaire faith in a literate electorate as the means to good government and in laissez-faire economics as a means to social harmony.

This utilitarian tradition was humanized by James Mill's son, John Stuart Mill, one of the most influential of mid-Victorian liberals. Whereas James Mill had been entirely pragmatic, his son tried to enhance more sophisticated values. He thought that civilization depended on a tiny minority of creative minds and on the free play of speculative intelligence. He detested conventional public opinion and feared that complete democracy, far from emancipating opinion, would make it more restrictive. Amid the dogmatic and strident voices of mid–19th-century nationalists, utopians, and revolutionaries, the quiet, if sometimes priggish, voice of mid-Victorian liberalism proved extremely influential in the ruling circles of Victorian England.

Accepting democracy as inevitable, John Stuart Mill expressed the still optimistic and progressive views of an intellectual elite. Without complete liberty of opinion, he insisted, civilizations ossify. The quality of progress results not merely from the blind forces of economic competition but from the free play of mind. The worth of the state in the long run is only the worth of the individuals composing it, and without people of genius society would become a "stagnant pool." This militant humanist, unlike his father, was aware of the dangers of even benevolent bureaucratic power and declared that a state that "dwarfs its men" is culturally insignificant.

Mill also advocated the legal and social emancipation of women, holding that ability was wasted by

John Stuart Mill, 1884. Library of Congres, Neg. Co. LC-USZ62-76491

mid-Victorian conventions. He believed that the masses could be educated into accepting the values of liberal civilization, but he defended private property and was as wary of rapid extensions of the franchise as of bureaucratic power.

In addition to his work in ethics and political philosophy, Mill also made important contributions to logic and the philosophy of science. In his enormously influential *A System of Logic* (1843), Mill made the fundamental distinction between deduction and induction, defined induction as the process for discovering and proving general propositions, and presented his "four methods of experimental inquiry" as the heart of the inductive method. These methods were, in fact, only an enlarged and refined version of Francis Bacon's tables of discovery.

Mill took the experience of the uniformity of nature as the warrant of induction. Here he reaffirmed the belief of Hume that it is possible to apply the principle of causation and the methods of physical science to moral and social phenomena. These may be so complex as to yield only "conditional predictions," but in this sense there are "social laws." Thus Comte and Mill agreed on the possibility of a genuine social science.

KARL MARX

In the 1840s a new generation of Hegelians — the so-called "left" or "young" Hegelians — became disillusioned with Hegel's philosophy as a result of the philosopher's open flirtation with political reaction in the *Philosophy of Right* and other texts. They came to regard Hegelian idealism as merely the philosophical window dressing of Prussian authoritarianism. From a similar point of view, Karl Marx (1818–83) famously criticized his fellow Germans for achieving in thought what other peoples — notably the

Karl Marx's views became the basis of modern Marxism. Henry Guttmann/ Hulton Archive/Getty Images

French—had accomplished in reality. It seemed unlikely that a philosophy such as Hegel's could ever serve progressive political ends.

The Young Hegelians—especially Bruno Bauer (1809–82) and David Friedrich Strauss (1808–74)—vigorously criticized Hegel's complacent defense of state religion and his monarchism, and they emphatically endorsed the ideal of a secular constitutional republic. In *The Essence of Christianity* and other works, Ludwig Feuerbach (1804–72), another Young Hegelian, tried to substitute an "anthropological humanism" for Hegel's speculative dialectic. Hegel's philosophy claimed primacy for the "idea," whereas Feuerbach tried to show, in an Enlightenment spirit, how thinking was a derivative or second-order activity with regard to human existence. German idealism claimed that concepts form the basis of existence or actually constitute reality. However, Feuerbach, stressing the materialist dimension of philosophy in a manner reminiscent of high Enlightenment materialism, reversed this claim. Instead, he contended that concrete human existence is fundamental. Ideas themselves are an outgrowth or efflux of man's nature as a sensuous, anthropological being. Feuerbach's method of "transformative criticism," which replaced the Hegelian "idea" with the notion of "man," had a significant impact on the development of Marx's philosophy.

Although a Young Hegelian during his student days, Marx soon developed significant philosophical and political differences with other members of the group. Already in his early, Rousseau-inspired work *On the Jewish Question,* Marx had emphasized that in the constitutional state desired by his fellow Left Hegelians, political problems would merely shift to another plane. Religion and bourgeois self-absorption, Marx argued, would merely be transposed to the private sphere of civil society. Society, moreover, would still be riven by the separation between bourgeois and citizen. Still under Hegel's influence, Marx believed that all such instances of separation or alienation must be transcended for human emancipation—as opposed to mere political emancipation—to be achieved.

Although the young Marx wished to supplant idealist dialectics with a sociohistorical approach, his initial deduction of the world-historical role of the proletariat was reminiscent of Hegel in its decidedly speculative and philosophical character:

> *A class must be formed which has radical chains, a class in civil society which is not a class of civil society, a class which is the dissolution of all classes, a sphere of society which has a universal character because its sufferings are universal, and which does not claim a particular redress because the wrong which is done to it is not a particular wrong but wrong in general.*

The philosophical project of German idealism, a reconciliation of idea and reality, thought and being, remained a primary inspiration for Marx. Nevertheless, Marx believed that Hegel, because of his speculative biases, had provided an inadequate grounding in reality for this utopian goal. Marx's concept of the proletariat would reveal how, practically speaking, this ideal could become reality. In 1843–44 Marx described communism in Hegelian terms as a dialectical transcendence of "alienation," an ultimate union between subject and object:

> *[Communism] is the genuine resolution of the conflict between man and nature and between man and man—the true resolution of the strife between existence and essence, between objectification and self-confirmation, between freedom and necessity, between the individual and the species. Communism*

is the riddle of history solved, and it knows itself to be this solution.

Thereafter, Marx became convinced that communism had less to do with "realizing philosophy" than with the laws of capitalist development. Correspondingly, traces of his early Hegelianism became less visible in his later work.

Marx's revolutionary fervour tended to harm his philosophical reputation in the West, and his philosophical achievement remains a matter of controversy. But certain Marxian ideas (some Hegelian in inspiration, some original) have endured. Among these are:

1. That society is a moving balance (dialectic) of antithetical forces that produce social change.
2. That there is no conflict between a rigid economic determinism and a program of revolutionary action.
3. That ideas (including philosophical theories) are not purely rational and thus cannot be independent of external circumstances but depend upon the nature of the social order in which they arise.

INDEPENDENT AND IRRATIONALIST MOVEMENTS

The end of the 19th century was marked by a flowering of many independent philosophical movements. Although by then Hegel had been nearly forgotten in Germany, a Hegelian renaissance was under way in England, led by T.H. Green (1836–82), F.H. Bradley (1846–1924), and Bernard Bosanquet (1848–1923). Bradley's *Appearance and Reality* (1893) constituted the high-water mark of the rediscovery of Hegel's dialectical method. In the United States, a strong reaction against idealism fostered the pragmatic movement, led by Charles Sanders Peirce (1839–1914) and William James (1842–1910). Peirce, a logician, held that the function of all inquiry is to eradicate doubt and that the meaning of a concept consists of its practical consequences. James transformed Peirce's pragmatic theory of meaning into a pragmatic theory of truth. In *The Will to Believe* (1897), he asserted that human beings have a right to believe even in the face of inconclusive evidence and that, because knowledge is essentially an instrument, the practical consequences of a belief are the real test of its truth: true beliefs are those that work. Meanwhile, in Austria, Franz Brentano (1838–1917), who taught at the University of Vienna from 1874 to 1895, and Alexius Meinong (1853–1920), who taught at Graz, Austria, were developing an empirical psychology and a theory of intentional objects (objects considered as the contents of a mental state) that were to have considerable influence upon the new movement of phenomenology.

It was not any of these late 19th-century developments, however, but rather the emphasis on the irrational, which started almost at the century's beginning, that gave the philosophy of the period its peculiar flavour. Hegel, despite his commitment to systematic metaphysics, had nevertheless carried on the Enlightenment tradition of faith in human rationality. But soon his influence was challenged from two different directions. One of Hegel's contemporaries, Arthur Schopenhauer, himself a German idealist and constructor of a bold and imaginative system, contradicted Hegel by asserting that the irrational is the truly real. And the Danish Christian thinker Søren Kierkegaard criticized what he considered the logical pretensions of the Hegelian system.

Kierkegaard, Schopenhauer, and, later in the 19th century, Nietzsche provided a new, nonrational conception of human nature. And they viewed the mind not as open to rational introspection but as dark, obscure, hidden, and deep. Above all they initiated a new style of philosophizing. Schopenhauer wrote like an 18th-century essayist, Kierkegaard was a master of the methods of irony and paradox, and Nietzsche used aphorism and epigram in a self-consciously literary manner. For them, the philosopher should be less a crabbed academician than a man of letters.

ARTHUR SCHOPENHAUER

For a short time Schopenhauer unsuccessfully competed with Hegel at the University of Berlin. Thereafter he withdrew to spend the rest of his life in battle against academic philosophy. His own system, though orderly and carefully worked out, was expressed in vivid and engaging language.

Schopenhauer's philosophy returned to the Kantian distinction between appearances and things-in-themselves, or between phenomena and noumena, to stress the limitations of reason. In his major philosophical work, *Die Welt als Wille und Vorstellung* (1819; *The World as Will and Representation*), Schopenhauer reiterated Kant's claim that, given the structure of human cognition, knowledge of things as they really are is impossible; the best that can be obtained are comparatively superficial representations of things.

But the most influential aspect of Schopenhauer's philosophy was his recasting of the concept of the will. He viewed the will as a quasi-mystical life force that underlay all of reality: "This word [will] indicates that which is the being-in-itself of everything in the world, and is the sole kernel of every phenomenon." Although the will remained inaccessible to ideas or concepts, its nature could be fathomed or glimpsed through nonrational aesthetic experience—an insight that was clearly indebted to Schelling's philosophy as well as to the romantic concept of "genius."

Although *The World as Will and Representation* had little effect when it was first published, Schopenhauer's pessimism—his devaluation of the capacities of the intellect and his corresponding conviction that reality is ultimately unknowable—became a virtual credo for a subsequent generation of European intellectuals whose hopes for democratic reform across the continent were dashed by the failure of the Revolutions of 1848. His belief in the ability of art, particularly music, to afford metaphysical insight profoundly influenced the aesthetic theories of the German composer Richard Wagner. And his philosophy of the will, as well as his stark view of reason as incapable of grasping the true nature of reality, had a considerable impact on the philosophy of Friedrich Nietzsche.

SØREN KIERKEGAARD

Kierkegaard's criticism of Hegel was an appeal to the concrete as against the abstract. He satirized Hegelian rationalism as a perfect example of "the academic in philosophy"—of detached, objective, abstract theorizing, and system building that was blind to the realities of human existence and to its subjective, living, emotional character. What a human being requires in life, said Kierkegaard, is not infinite inquiry but the boldness of resolute decision and commitment. The human essence is not to be found in thinking but in the existential conditions of emotional life, in anxiety and despair. The titles of three of Kierkegaard's books—*Frygt og baeven* (1843; *Fear and Trembling*), *Begrebet angest* (1844; *The Concept of Anxiety*), and *Sygdommen til døden* (1849; *The Sickness unto*

Death)—indicate his preoccupation with states of consciousness quite unlike cognition.

Kierkegaard frequently wrote pseudonymously and ironically, self-consciously adopting a literary rather than a scientific idiom in which he mercilessly indicted his contemporaries for their faithlessness and ethical conformity. As a Protestant thinker, Kierkegaard believed he was returning to the concerns of Pauline Christianity, and he viewed the *Confessions* of St. Augustine (354–430) as an important literary precedent. Only by probing the recesses of his own inner self or subjectivity can the individual accede to truth. In one of his best-known works, *Fear and Trembling*, he reconstructed the biblical tale of Abraham, praising the protagonist's "teleological suspension of the ethical" for his willingness to sacrifice his only son on the basis of his unshakable faith. Kierkegaard's stress on the forlornness of the human condition, as well as on the absence of certainty concerning the possibility of salvation, made him an important forerunner of 20th-century existentialism.

FRIEDRICH NIETZSCHE

As a youthful disciple of Schopenhauer, Friedrich Nietzsche was influenced by the older philosopher's critique of reason and by his suggestion that art, as an expression of genius, afforded a glimpse of being-in-itself. Trained as a classicist, Nietzsche's encounter with Attic tragedy led him to a reevaluation of Greek culture that would have a momentous effect on modern thought and literature. In a pathbreaking dissertation that was ultimately published in 1872 as *Die Geburt der Tragödie* (1872; *The Birth of Tragedy*), Nietzsche claimed that the dramas of Aeschylus and Sophocles represented the high point of Greek culture, whereas the philosophy of Plato and Platonism

Friedrich Nietzsche, 1888. Louis Held/Deutsche Fotothek, Dresden

constituted a decline. Nietzsche's study culminated in a withering critique of Socrates and the Western philosophical tradition engendered by his method of logical analysis and argumentation—*elenchos*, or dialectic. "Our whole modern world," Nietzsche laments, "is caught in the net of Alexandrian [Hellenistic] culture and recognizes as its ideal the man of theory, equipped with the highest cognitive powers, working in the service of science, and whose archetype and progenitor is Socrates."

Nietzsche was disturbed by the Enlightenment's unswerving allegiance to the concept of scientific truth. In a brilliant early text, *Über Wahrheit und Lüge im aussermoralischen Sinn* (1873; *On Truth and Lies in a Non-Moral Sense*), he offered many insightful observations about the vocation of philosophy that would ultimately find their way into his mature thought of the 1880s. The will to philosophy, with its pretensions to objectivity, should not be taken at face value, suggests Nietzsche, for its veil of impartiality conceals an array of specific biological functions. The intellect is a practical instrument employed by the human species to master a complex and hostile environment. Despite pious insistences to the contrary by philosophers, there is nothing sacrosanct about their vocation. "What is a word?" Nietzsche asks. "It is the copy in sound of a nerve stimulus." Like other biological phenomena, thought stands in the service of life as a means of self-preservation. "As a means for the preserving of the individual, the intellect unfolds its principle powers in dissimulation, which is the means by which weaker, less robust individuals preserve themselves," Nietzsche observes.

Nietzsche couples these criticisms with astute observations concerning the relationship between philosophy and language. For centuries philosophers have claimed that they possess access to absolute truth. Yet such pretensions belie the extent to which philosophical discourse, like all human communication, is mediated by the rhetorical and representational contingencies of language. With language as an instrument or intermediary apparatus, human conceptual access to the "in-itself," or real being, of objects is unavoidably mediated, hence never direct or pristine. Without the rhetorical approximations of metaphor, trope, and figuration, the philosophical enterprise would languish and wither. Truth, regarded by the philosophers' guild as something magical and sacred, is, claims Nietzsche, merely a series of metaphors, or imprecise rhetorical approximations, mobilized to achieve a certain effect or a set of desired ends. It is

> *a movable host of metaphors, metonymies, and anthropomorphisms: in short, a sum of human relations which have been poetically and rhetorically intensified, transferred, and embellished, and which, after long usage, seem to a people to be fixed, canonical, and blind. Truths are illusions which we have forgotten are illusions.*

Ultimately, and contrary to what philosophers have perennially contended, the relationship between concepts and the things they designate, far from being necessary or intrinsic, is merely a matter of convention and habit. Truth does not yield a "view from nowhere." As Nietzsche insinuates, it inevitably involves an "anthropomorphic" dimension: it is both a reflection of custom and a projection of human need. Nietzsche's later doctrine of the "will to power"—which characterizes philosophy, like all human undertakings, as a quest for world mastery—systematized many of these early insights concerning the finite and conditioned nature of truth. His emphasis on truth's inescapable linguistic and rhetorical components would, a century later, profoundly influenced the views of the French philosophers Michel Foucault (1926–84) and Jacques Derrida (1930–2004).

Despite his questioning of traditional philosophical concepts such as truth, Nietzsche remained committed to the goals of serious philosophical inquiry. Indeed, his prodigious philosophical musings are informed by two precepts handed down by Socrates: (1) the unexamined life is not worth living; and (2) virtue is a kind of knowledge (that is, being virtuous consists of knowing what virtue is in general and what the virtues are in particular). Although Nietzsche emphatically rejected Plato's theory that the properties of earthly objects are merely imperfect copies of abstract, celestial Forms, he remained convinced that wisdom, and therefore possession of the truth, was the key to human flourishing. Nor did his later "perspectivism"—the idea that all knowledge is situated and partial—amount to a shallow relativism. Instead, Nietzsche intended his "transvaluation of all values"—his reversal or inversion of all received conceptions of truth—as a way station on the path to a set of higher, more robust and affirmative ethical ideals. The same impassioned concern for the welfare of the soul that one finds in Socrates and Plato one also discovers in Nietzsche. Moreover, Nietzsche's philosophy was motivated at every turn by Aristotle's distinction between mere life and the "good life"—a life lived in accordance with virtue.

Not only did Nietzsche never relinquish his interest in "first philosophy," but he approached metaphysical problems in a manner that was remarkably consistent and rigorous. To be sure, his aphoristic and fragmentary writing style makes it difficult to develop a systematic interpretation of his thought. It is clear, however, that

Nietzsche embraced the fundamental questions of metaphysics and sought to provide them with compelling and original answers. After all, were not his doctrines of the will to power and "eternal recurrence"—the idea that life must be lived emphatically, as if one might be condemned in perpetuity to repeat a given action—in essence attempts to come to grips with the essential nature of being and, as such, metaphysics at its purest? What was his theory of the "superman"—of a superior being or nature who transcends the timidity and foibles of the merely human—if not an earnest attempt to redefine virtue or the good life in an era in which cultural philistinism seemed to have gained the upper hand? And what motivated Nietzsche's perspectivism if not a desire to arrive at a less-limited, more robust understanding of the nature of truth in all its richness and multiplicity?

In *Lieder des Prinzen Vogelfrei* (1887; *The Gay Science*), Nietzsche proclaims that

> it is still a metaphysical faith upon which our faith in knowl-
> edge rests—that even we knowers today, we godless
> anti-metaphysicians still take our fire from the flame lit by a
> faith that is thousands of years old, that Christian faith which
> was also the faith of Plato, that God is truth, that truth is
> divine.

This passage could hardly have been written by someone who was not a "lover of wisdom" (i.e., a philosopher).

WILHELM DILTHEY AND HENRI BERGSON

Nietzsche's skepticism about the capacities of reason, as well as his belief in the inherent limitations of a predominantly scientific culture, was shared by many late

19th-century thinkers and writers. One consequence of his wide-ranging influence was the popularity of the concept of "life" as an antidote to the rise of scientific positivism.

In Germany an early opponent of this trend, the philosopher Wilhelm Dilthey (1833–1911), argued that, whereas the natural sciences aimed to explain all of physical reality in terms of unchanging, general laws, the "human sciences" (*Geisteswissenschaften*), such as history, sought to capture unique individuals or events from the past. The latter undertaking, therefore, required a different epistemological approach. Dilthey distinguished between the styles of explanation characteristic of the natural sciences and the human sciences: the one seeks objective, impersonal, causal knowledge, the other seeks "understanding" (*Verstehen*), which is ultimately based on the motivations and intentions of historical actors. "Understanding always has as its object something individual," argued Dilthey in *Der Aufbau der geschichtlichen Welt in den Geisteswissenschaften* (1910; *The Structure of the Historical World in the Human Sciences*).

A similar movement was afoot in France under the inspiration of Henri Bergson (1859–1941), whose philosophy of vitalism sought to contrast the subjective notion of "duration" with the objective conception of time proper to the natural sciences. As he remarked in *L'Évolution créatrice* (1907; *Creative Evolution*): "Anticipated time is not mathematical time . . . It coincides with duration, which is not subject to being prolonged or retracted at will. It is no longer something thought but something lived." In France Bergson's views made few inroads among more traditional philosophers, in part because of the mechanistic orientation of Cartesianism and in part because of a general sympathy toward science inherited from the Enlightenment. Instead, his influence was greatest among novelists (e.g., Marcel Proust, 1871–1922) and political theorists (e.g., Charles Péguy, 1873–1914, and Georges Sorel, 1847–1922).

In Germany the corresponding school, known as *Lebensphilosophie* ("philosophy of life"), began to take on aspects of a political ideology in the years immediately preceding World War I. The work of Hans Driesch (1867–1941) and Ludwig Klages (1872–1956), for example, openly condemned the superficial intellectualism of Western civilization. In associating "reason" with the shortcomings of "civilization" and "the West," *Lebensphilosophie* spurred many German thinkers to reject intellection in favour of the irrational forces of blood and life.

CHAPTER 5

CONTEMPORARY PHILOSOPHY

Philosophy in the 20th century was characterized by a sharpening of the divisions between two longstanding traditions. The tradition of clear logical analysis, inaugurated by Locke and Hume, dominated the English-speaking world, whereas a speculative and broadly historical tradition, begun by Hegel but later diverging radically from him, held sway on the European continent. From the early decades of the century, the substantive as well as stylistic differences between the two approaches—known after World War II as analytic and Continental philosophy, respectively—gradually became more pronounced, and until the 1990s few serious attempts were made to find common ground between them.

Other less significant currents in 20th-century philosophy were the speculative philosophies of John Dewey (1859–1952) of the United States and Alfred North Whitehead (1861–1947) of England—each of whom evades easy classification—and the philosophical Marxism practiced in the Soviet Union and eastern Europe until the collapse of communism there in 1990–91.

JOHN DEWEY AND ALFRED NORTH WHITEHEAD

John Dewey was a generalist who stressed the unity, interrelationship, and organicity of all forms of philosophical knowledge. He is chiefly notable for the fact that his conception of philosophy stressed so powerfully the notions of practicality and moral purpose. One of the guiding aims of Dewey's philosophizing was the effort to find the same warranted assertibility for ethical and political judgements as for scientific ones. Philosophy, he said, should be oriented not to professional pride but to human need.

Dewey's approach to the social problems of the 20th century emphasized not revolution but the continuous application of the intellect to social affairs. He believed in social planning—conscious, intelligent intervention to produce desirable social change—and he proposed a new "experimentalism" as a guide to enlightened public action to promote the aims of a democratic community. His

Alfred North Whitehead.

pragmatic social theory is the first major political philosophy produced by modern liberal democracy.

For Whitehead, in contrast, philosophy was primarily metaphysics, or "speculative philosophy," which he described as the effort "to frame a coherent, logical, necessary system of general ideas in terms of which every element of our experience can be interpreted." Whitehead's philosophy was thus an attempt to survey the world with a large generality of understanding, an end toward which his great trilogy, *Science and the Modern World* (1925), *Process and Reality* (1929), and *Adventures of Ideas* (1933), was directed.

MARXIST THOUGHT

The framework of 19th-century Marxism, augmented by philosophical suggestions from Vladimir Ilich Lenin (1870–1924), served as the starting point of all philosophizing in the Soviet Union and its Eastern European satellites. Much of Lenin's thinking was also devoted to more practical issues, however, such as tactics of violence and the role of the Communist Party in bringing about and consolidating the proletarian revolution. Later Marxism continued this practical concern, largely because it retained the basic Marxist conception of what philosophy is and ought to be. Marxism (like pragmatism) assimilated theoretical issues to practical needs. It asserted the basic unity of theory and practice by finding that the function of the former was to serve the latter. Marx and Lenin both held that theory was always, in fact, expressive of class interests. Consequently, they wished philosophy to be transformed into a tool for furthering the class struggle. The task of philosophy was not abstractly to discover the truth but concretely to forge the intellectual weapons of the proletariat. Thus, philosophy became inseparable from ideology.

VLADIMIR ILICH LENIN

Vladimir Ilich Lenin's interpretation of Marx's philosophy, realized in the Soviet Union by Lenin and developed by Joseph Stalin (1879–1953), was entirely authoritarian. According to Marx and his colleague Friedrich Engels (1820–95), the revolution could occur in Russia only after the bourgeois phase of production had "contradicted" the tsarist order, but Lenin was determined to take advantage of the opportunities provided by the upheaval of World War I to settle accounts directly with the "accursed heritage of serfdom." In the Russian Revolution of 1917, he engineered a coup that secured the support of the peasantry and the industrial workers. He also adopted the revolutionary theorist Leon Trotsky's idea of a "permanent revolution" from above by a small revolutionary elite.

Already in *Chto delat?* (1902; *What Is to Be Done?*), Lenin had argued that an educated elite had to direct the proletarian revolution, and, when he came to power, he dissolved the constituent assembly and ruled through a "revolutionary and democratic dictatorship supported by the state power of the armed workers." In asserting the need for an elite of professional revolutionaries to seize power, Lenin reverted to Marx's program in *Manifest der Kommunistischen Partei* (1848; commonly known as *The Communist Manifesto*) rather than conform to the fated pattern of economic development worked out by Marx in *Das Kapital* ("Capital"), 3 vol. (1867, 1885, 1894).

In 1921 he further adapted theory to the times. His New Economic Policy sanctioned the development of a class of prosperous peasantry to keep the economy

Vladimir Ilich Lenin, 1918. Tass/Sovfoto

viable. For Lenin always thought in terms of world revolution, and, in spite of the failure of the Marxists in central Europe and the defeat of the Red armies in Poland, he died in the expectation of a global sequel. Thus, in *Imperializm, kak vysshaya stadiya kapitalizma* (1917; *Imperialism, the Latest Stage in the Development of Capitalism*), he had extended the class war into an inevitable conflict between European imperialism and the colonial peoples involved. He had been influenced by *Imperialism, a Study* (1902), by the English historian J.A. Hobson (1858–1940), which alleged that decadent capitalism was bound to turn from glutted markets at home to exploit the toil of "reluctant and unassimilated peoples."

GYÖRGY LUKÁCS AND ANTONIO GRAMSCI

Many revisionist interpreters of Marx tended toward anarchism (the doctrine that government is both harmful and unnecessary), stressing the Hegelian and utopian elements of his theory. The Hungarian philosopher György Lukács (1885–1971), for example, and the German-born American philosopher Herbert Marcuse (1898–1979), who fled Nazi Germany in 1934, won some following in the mid-20th century among those in revolt against both authoritarian "peoples' democracies" and the diffused capitalism and meritocracy of the managerial welfare state. In *Geschichte und Klassenbewusstsein* (1923; *History and Class Consciousness*), a neo-Hegelian work, Lukács claimed that only the intuition of the proletariat can properly apprehend the totality of history. But world revolution is contingent, not inevitable, and Marxism is an instrument, not a prediction. Lukács renounced this heresy after residence in the Soviet Union under Stalin, but he maintained influence through literary and dramatic criticism. After the Soviet leader Nikita Khrushchev

(1894–1971) denounced Stalin in 1956, Lukács advocated peaceful coexistence and intellectual rather than political subversion. In *Wider den missverstandenen Realismus* (1963; *The Meaning of Contemporary Realism*), he again related Marx to Hegel and even to Aristotle, against the Stalinist claim that Marx had made a radically new departure. Lukács's neo-Hegelian insights, strikingly expressed, appealed to those eager to salvage the more humane aspects of Marxism and to promote revolution, even against a modified capitalism and social democracy, by intellectual rather than political means.

The Italian communist philosopher Antonio Gramsci (1891–1937) deployed a vivid rhetorical talent in attacking existing society. Gramsci was alarmed that the proletariat was being assimilated by the capitalist order. He took his stand on the already obsolescent Marxist doctrine of irreconcilable class war between bourgeois and proletariat. He aimed to unmask the bourgeois idea of liberty and to replace parliaments by an "implacable machine" of workers' councils, which would destroy the current social order through a dictatorship of the proletariat. "Democracy," he wrote, "is our worst enemy. We must be ready to fight it because it blurs the clear separation of classes."

Not only would parliamentary democracy and established law be unmasked, but culture too would be transformed. A workers' civilization, with its great industry, large cities, and "tumultuous and intense life," would create a new civilization with new poetry, art, drama, fashions, and language. Gramsci insisted that the old culture should be destroyed and that education should be wrenched from the grip of the ruling classes and the church.

But this militant revolutionary was also a utopian. He turned bitterly hostile to Stalin's regime, for he believed, like Engels, that the dictatorship of the workers' state would wither away. "We do not wish," he wrote, "to freeze the dictatorship." Following world revolution, a classless society would emerge, and humankind would be free to master nature instead of being involved in a class war. Gramsci was arrested by the Fascist government of Benito Mussolini (1883–1945) in 1926 and spent the next 11 years in prison, dying shortly after his release for medical care in 1937.

CRITICAL THEORY

Critical theory, a broad-based Marxist-oriented approach to the study of society, was first developed in the 1920s by the philosophers Max Horkheimer (1895–1973), Theodor Adorno (1903–69), and Herbert Marcuse at the Institute for Social Research in Frankfurt, Ger. They and other members of the Frankfurt School, as this group came to be called, fled Germany after the Nazis came to power in 1933. The institute was relocated to Columbia University in the United States and remained there until 1949, when it was reestablished in Frankfurt. The most prominent representatives of the Frankfurt School and of critical theory from the mid-20th century were Marcuse and Jürgen Habermas.

The question initially addressed by critical theorists was why the working classes in advanced capitalist countries were generally unmotivated to press for radical social change in their own interests. They attempted to develop a theory of capitalist social relations and analyze the various forms of cultural and ideological oppression arising from them. Critical theorists also undertook major studies of fascism and later of dictatorial communist regimes. After World War II, during the era of the Cold War, critical theorists viewed the world as divided

Herbert Marcuse was a member of the Frankfurt School of critical social analysis, whose Marxist and Freudian theories influenced leftist student movements. Keystone/Hulton Archive/Getty Images

between two inherently oppressive models of social development. In these historical circumstances, questions concerning human liberation—what it consists of and how it can be attained—seemed especially urgent.

In *Dialektik der Aufklärung* (1947; *Dialectic of Enlightenment*), Horkheimer and Adorno argued that the celebration of reason by thinkers of the 18th-century Enlightenment had led to the development of technologically sophisticated but oppressive and inhumane modes of governance, exemplified in the 20th century by fascism and totalitarianism. In works published in the 1950s and '60s, Marcuse attacked both the ideological conformism of managerial capitalism and the bureaucratic oppression of the communist "peoples' democracies." In his best-known and most influential work, *One-Dimensional Man* (1964), he argued that the modern capitalist "affluent" society oppresses even those who are successful within it while maintaining their complacency through the ersatz satisfactions of consumer culture. By cultivating such shallow forms of experience and by blocking critical understanding of the real workings of the system, the affluent society condemns its members to a "one-dimensional" existence of intellectual and spiritual poverty. Seeing human freedom as everywhere in retreat, Marcuse later transferred the redeeming mission of the proletariat to a relative fringe of radical minorities, including (in the United States) the student New Left and militant groups such as the Black Panther Party.

Critical theorists initially believed that they could liberate people from false beliefs, or "false consciousness," and in particular from ideologies that served to maintain the political and economic status quo, by pointing out to them that they had acquired these beliefs in irrational ways (e.g., through indoctrination). In the end, however, some theorists, notably Marcuse, wondered whether the forces tending to promote ideological conformity in modern capitalist societies had so compromised the perceptions and reasoning powers of most individuals that no rational critique would ever be effective.

NON-MARXIST POLITICAL PHILOSOPHY

Notwithstanding John Dewey's important contributions to the theory of democracy, political philosophy in English-speaking countries in the first half of the 20th century was inhibited to some extent by the advent in the 1920s of logical positivism, a doctrine that conceived of knowledge claims on the model of the hypotheses of natural science. According to the simplest version of logical positivism, genuine knowledge claims can be divided into two groups: (1) those that can be verified or falsified on the basis of observation, or sense experience (empirical claims); and (2) those that are true or false simply by virtue of the conventional meanings assigned to the words they contain (tautologies or contradictions), along with their logical implications. All other claims, including the evaluative assertions made by traditional political and ethical philosophers, are literally meaningless, hence not worth discussing. A complementary view held by some logical positivists was that an evaluative assertion, properly understood, is not a statement of fact but either an expression of the speaker's attitude (e.g., of approval or disapproval) or an imperative—a speech act aimed at influencing the behaviour of others. This view of the language of ethical and political philosophy tended to limit serious study in those fields until the 1960s, when logical positivism came to be regarded as simplistic in its conceptions of linguistic meaning and scientific practice.

There were, in addition to Dewey, other exceptions to this trend, the most notable being the German-born philosopher Hannah Arendt (1906–75), who became a U.S. citizen in 1951. In the second half of the 20th century, American philosopher John Rawls (1921–2002) developed a sophisticated defense of political liberalism, which provoked challenging responses from libertarians, communitarians, and others.

HANNAH ARENDT

Hannah Arendt's reputation as a major political thinker was established by her *Origins of Totalitarianism* (1951), which also treated 19th-century anti-Semitism, imperialism, and racism. Arendt viewed the growth of totalitarianism as the outcome of the disintegration of the traditional nation-state. She argued that totalitarian regimes, through their pursuit of raw political power and their neglect of material or utilitarian considerations, had revolutionized the social structure and made contemporary politics nearly impossible to predict.

The Human Condition, published in 1958, was a wide-ranging and systematic treatment of what Arendt called the *vita activa* (Latin: "active life"). She defended the classical ideals of work, citizenship, and political action against what she considered a debased obsession with mere welfare. Like most of her work, it owed a great deal to the philosophical style of her former teacher, Martin Heidegger (1889–1976).

In a highly controversial work, *Eichmann in Jerusalem* (1963), based on her reportage of the trial of the Nazi war criminal Adolf Eichmann in 1961, Arendt argued that Eichmann's crimes resulted not from a wicked or depraved character but from sheer "thoughtlessness":

Hannah Arendt gained prestige as a major political force with her critical writing on Jewish affairs and her study of totalitarianism. Apic/Hulton Archive/Getty Images

he was simply an ambitious bureaucrat who failed to reflect on the enormity of what he was doing. His role in the mass extermination of Jews epitomized "the fearsome, word-and-thought-defying banality of evil" that had spread across Europe at the time. Arendt's refusal to recognize Eichmann as "inwardly" evil prompted fierce denunciations from both Jewish and non-Jewish intellectuals.

JOHN RAWLS

The publication of John Rawls's *A Theory of Justice* (1971) spurred a revival of interest in the philosophical foundations of political liberalism. The viability of liberalism was thereafter a major theme of political philosophy in English-speaking countries.

According to the American philosopher Thomas Nagel, liberalism is the conjunction of two ideals: (1) individuals should have liberty of thought and speech and wide freedom to live their lives as they choose (so long as they do not harm others in certain ways), and (2) through majority rule individuals in any society should be able to determine the laws by which they are governed and should not be so unequal in status or wealth that they have unequal opportunities to participate in democratic decision making. Various traditional and modern versions of liberalism differ from each other in their interpretation of these ideals and in the relative importance they assign to them.

In *A Theory of Justice*, Rawls observed that a necessary condition of justice in any society is that each individual should be the equal bearer of certain rights that cannot be disregarded under any circumstances, even if doing so would advance the general welfare or satisfy the demands of a majority. This condition cannot

John Rawls. Harvard University News Office

be met by utilitarianism, because that ethical theory would countenance forms of government in which the greater happiness of a majority is achieved by neglecting the rights and interests of a minority. Hence, utilitarianism is unsatisfactory as a theory of justice, and another theory must be sought.

According to Rawls, a just society is one whose major political, social, and economic institutions, taken together, satisfy the following two principles:

1. Each person has an equal claim to a scheme of basic rights and liberties that is the maximum consistent with the same scheme for all.

2. Social and economic inequalities are permissible only if: (a) they confer the greatest benefit to the least-advantaged members of society, and (b) they are attached to positions and offices open to all under conditions of fair equality of opportunity.

The basic rights and liberties in principle 1 include the rights and liberties of democratic citizenship, such as the right to vote; the right to run for office in free elections; freedom of speech, assembly, and religion; the right to a fair trial; and, more generally, the right to the rule of law. Principle 1 is accorded strict priority over principle 2, which regulates social and economic inequalities.

Principle 2 combines two ideals. The first, known as the "difference principle," requires that any unequal distribution of social or economic goods (e.g., wealth) must be such that the least advantaged members of society would be better off under that distribution than they would be under any other distribution consistent with principle 1, including an equal distribution. (A slightly unequal distribution might benefit the least advantaged by encouraging greater overall productivity.) The second ideal is meritocracy, understood in an extremely demanding way. According to Rawls, fair equality of opportunity obtains in a society when all persons with the same native talent (genetic inheritance) and the same degree of ambition have the same prospects for success in all competitions for positions that confer special economic and social advantages.

Why suppose with Rawls that justice requires an approximately egalitarian redistribution of social and economic goods? After all, a person who prospers in a market economy might plausibly say, "I earned my wealth. Therefore, I am entitled to keep it." But how one fares in a market economy depends on luck as well as effort. There is the luck of being in the right place at the right time and of benefiting from unpredictable shifts in supply and demand, but there is also the luck of being born with greater or lesser intelligence and other desirable traits, along with the luck of growing up in a nurturing environment. No one can take credit for this kind of luck, but it decisively influences how one fares in the many competitions by which social and economic goods are distributed. Indeed, sheer brute luck is so thoroughly intermixed with the contributions one makes to one's own success (or failure) that it is ultimately impossible to distinguish what a person is responsible for from what he is not. Given this fact, Rawls urged, the only plausible justification of inequality is that it serves to render everyone better off, especially those who have the least.

Rawls tried to accommodate his theory of justice to what he took to be the important fact that reasonable people disagree deeply about the nature of morality and the good life and will continue to do so in any nontyrannical society that respects freedom of speech. He aimed to render his theory noncommittal on these controversial matters and to posit a set of principles of justice that all reasonable persons could accept as valid, despite their disagreements.

CRITIQUES OF PHILOSOPHICAL LIBERALISM

Despite its wide appeal, Rawls's liberal egalitarianism soon faced challengers. An early conservative rival was libertarianism. According to this view, because each person is literally the sole rightful owner of himself, no one has property rights in anyone else (no person can own another person), and no one owes anything to anyone else. By "appropriating" unowned things, an individual may acquire over them full private ownership rights, which he may give away or exchange. One has the right to do whatever one chooses with whatever one legitimately owns, as long as one does not harm others in specified ways (i.e., by coercion, force, violence, fraud, theft, extortion, or physical damage to another's property). According to libertarians, Rawlsian liberal egalitarianism is unjust because it would allow (indeed, require) the state to redistribute social and economic goods without their owners' consent, in violation of their private ownership rights.

The most spirited and sophisticated presentation of the libertarian critique was *Anarchy, State, and Utopia* (1974), by the American philosopher Robert Nozick (1938–2002). Nozick also argued that a "minimal state,"

Robert Nozick. Harvard University News Office

one that limited its activities to the enforcement of people's basic libertarian rights, could have arisen in a hypothetical "state of nature" through a process in which no one's basic libertarian rights are violated. He regarded this demonstration as a refutation of anarchism, the doctrine that the state is inherently unjustified.

Rawls's theory of justice was challenged from other theoretical perspectives as well. Adherents of communitarianism, such as Michael Sandel and Michael Walzer, urged that the shared understanding of a community concerning how it is appropriate to live should outweigh the abstract and putatively impartial requirements of universal justice. Even liberal egalitarians criticized some aspects of Rawls's theory. Ronald Dworkin, for example, argued that understanding egalitarian justice requires striking the correct balance between an individual's responsibility for his own life and society's collective responsibility to provide genuine equal opportunity for all citizens.

ANALYTIC PHILOSOPHY

As noted earlier, contemporary analytic philosophy—also sometimes called "Anglo-American" philosophy (a term that is no longer culturally or geographically accurate)—is a descendant of the tradition of logical analysis inaugurated by the British empiricists, particularly Locke and Hume. It is difficult to give a precise definition of analytic philosophy, however, because it is not so much a specific doctrine as an overlapping set of approaches to philosophical problems. Its origin at the turn of the 20th century is often located in the work of two English philosophers, G.E. Moore (1873–1958) and Bertrand Russell (1872–1970).

The development of analytic philosophy was significantly influenced by the creation of symbolic (or mathematical) logic at the beginning of the century.

Although there are anticipations of this kind of logic in the Stoics, its modern forms are without exact parallel in Western thought, a fact that is made apparent by its close affinities with mathematics and science. Many philosophers thus regarded the combination of logic and science as a model that philosophical inquiry should follow, though others rejected the model or minimized its usefulness for dealing with philosophical problems. The 20th century thus witnessed the development of two diverse streams of analysis, one emphasizing formal (logical) techniques and the other informal (ordinary-language) ones. There were, of course, many philosophers whose work was influenced by both approaches. Although analysis can in principle be applied to any subject matter, its central focus for most of the century was language, especially the notions of meaning and reference. Ethics, aesthetics, religion, and law also were fields of interest, though to a lesser degree. The last quarter of the century exhibited a profound shift in emphasis from the topics of meaning and reference to issues about the human mind, including the nature of mental processes such as thinking, judging, perceiving, believing, and intending, as well as the products or objects of such processes, including representations, meanings, and visual images. At the same time, intensive work continued on the theory of reference, and the results obtained in that domain were transferred to the analysis of mind. Both formalist and informalist approaches exhibited this shift in interest.

THE FORMALIST TRADITION

Russell, whose general approach would be adopted by philosophers in the formalist tradition, was a major influence on those who believed that philosophical problems could be clarified, if not solved, by using the technical equipment of formal logic and who saw the physical sciences as the only means of gaining knowledge of the world. They regarded philosophy—if as a science at all—as a deductive and a priori enterprise on a par with mathematics. Russell's contributions to this side of the analytic tradition have been important and, in great part, lasting.

LOGICAL ATOMISM

The first major development in the formalist tradition was a metaphysical theory known as logical atomism, which was derived from Russell's work in mathematical logic. His work, in turn, was based in part on early notebooks written before World War I by his former pupil Ludwig Wittgenstein (1889–1953). In "The Philosophy of Logical Atomism," a monograph published in 1918, Russell gave credit to Wittgenstein for supplying "many of the theories" contained in it. Wittgenstein had joined the Austrian army when the war broke out, and Russell had been out of contact with him ever since. Wittgenstein thus did not become aware of Russell's version of logical atomism until after the war. Wittgenstein's polished and extremely sophisticated version appeared in the *Tractatus Logico-Philosophicus,* which he wrote during the war but did not publish until 1922.

Both Russell and Wittgenstein believed that mathematical logic could reveal the basic structure of reality, a structure that is hidden beneath the cloak of ordinary language. In their view, the new logic showed that the world is made up of simple, or "atomic," facts, which in turn are made up of particular objects. Atomic facts are complex, mind-independent features of reality, such as the fact that a particular rock is white or the fact that the Moon is a satellite of the Earth. As Wittgenstein says in the *Tractatus,* "The world is determined by the facts, and by their being *all* the facts." Both Russell and Wittgenstein held that the basic propositions of logic, which Wittgenstein called "elementary propositions," refer to atomic facts. There is thus an immediate connection between formal languages, such as the logical system of Russell's *Principia Mathematica* (written with Alfred North Whitehead and published between 1910 and 1913), and the structure of the real world: elementary propositions represent atomic facts, which are constituted by particular objects, which are the meanings of logically proper names. Russell differed from Wittgenstein in that he held that the meanings of proper names are "sense data," or immediate perceptual experiences, rather than particular objects. Furthermore, for Wittgenstein but not for Russell, elementary propositions are connected to the world by being structurally isomorphic to atomic facts (i.e., by being a "picture" of them). Wittgenstein's view thus came to be known as the "picture theory" of meaning.

Logical atomism rested on many theses. It was realistic, as distinct from idealistic, in its contention that there are mind-independent facts. But it presupposed that language is mind-dependent (i.e., that language would not exist unless there were sentient beings who used sounds and marks to refer and to communicate). Logical atomism was thus a dualistic metaphysics that described both the structure of the world and the conditions that any particular language must satisfy to represent it. Although its career was brief, its guiding principle—that philosophy should be scientific and grounded in mathematical logic—was widely acknowledged throughout the century.

Logical Positivism

Logical positivism was developed in the early 1920s by a group of Austrian intellectuals, mostly scientists and mathematicians, who named their association the Wiener

Kreis (Vienna Circle). The logical positivists accepted the logical atomist conception of philosophy as properly scientific and grounded in mathematical logic. By "scientific," however, they had in mind the classical empiricism handed down from Locke and Hume, in particular the view that all factual knowledge is based on experience. Unlike logical atomists, the logical positivists, as noted earlier, held that only logic, mathematics, and the special sciences can make statements that are meaningful, or cognitively significant. They thus regarded metaphysical, religious, ethical, literary, and aesthetic pronouncements as literally nonsense. Significantly, because logical atomism was a metaphysics purporting to convey true information about the structure of reality, it too was disavowed. The positivists also held that there is a fundamental distinction to be made between "analytic" statements (such as "All husbands are married"), which can be known to be true independently of any experience, and "synthetic" statements (such as "It is raining now"), which are knowable only through observation.

The main proponents of logical positivism—Rudolf Carnap (1891–1970), Herbert Feigl (1902–88), Philipp Frank (1884–1966), and Gustav Bergmann (1906–87)—all immigrated to the United States from Germany and Austria to escape Nazism. Their influence on American philosophy was profound, and, with various modifications after the 1960s, logical positivism was still a vital force on the American scene at the beginning of the 21st century.

NATURALIZED EPISTEMOLOGY

The philosophical psychology and philosophy of mind developed since the 1950s by the American philosopher Willard Van Orman Quine (1908–2000), known generally as naturalized epistemology, was influenced both by Russell's work in logic and by logical positivism. Quine's philosophy forms a comprehensive system that is scientistic, empiricist, and behaviourist. Indeed, for Quine, the basic task of an empiricist philosophy is simply to describe how our scientific theories about the world—as well as our prescientific, or intuitive, picture of it—are derived from experience. As he wrote:

> *The stimulation of his sensory receptors is all the evidence anybody has had to go on, ultimately, in arriving at his picture of the world. Why not just see how this construction really proceeds? Why not settle for psychology?*

Although Quine shared the logical postivists' scientism and empiricism, he crucially differed from them in rejecting the traditional analytic-synthetic distinction. For Quine, this distinction is ill-founded because it is not required by any adequate psychological account of how scientific (or prescientific) theories are formulated. Quine's views had an enormous impact on analytic philosophy, and until his death at the end of the century he was generally regarded as the dominant figure in the movement.

THEORIES IN THE PHILOSOPHY OF MIND

Logical positivism and naturalized epistemology were forms of materialism. Beginning about 1970, these approaches were applied to the human mind, giving rise to three general viewpoints: identity theory, functionalism, and eliminative materialism. Identity theory is the view that mental states are identical to physical states of the brain. According to functionalism, a particular mental state is any type of (physical) state that plays a certain causal role with respect to other mental and physical states. For example, pain can be functionally defined as any state that is an effect of events such as cuts and burns and that is a cause of mental states such as fear and behaviour such as saying "Ouch!" Eliminative materialism is the view that the familiar categories of "folk psychology"—such as belief, intention, and desire—do not refer to anything real. In other words, there are no such things as beliefs, intentions, or desires. Instead, there is simply neural activity in the brain. According to the eliminative materialist, a modern scientific account of the mind no more requires the categories of folk psychology than modern chemistry requires the discarded notion of phlogiston. A complete account of human mental experience can be achieved simply by describing how the brain operates.

The Informalist Tradition

Generally speaking, philosophers in the informalist tradition viewed philosophy as an autonomous activity that should acknowledge the importance of logic and science but not treat either or both as models for dealing with conceptual problems. The 20th century witnessed the development of three such approaches, each of which had sustained influence: common sense philosophy, ordinary language philosophy, and speech act theory.

Common Sense Philosophy

Originating as a reaction against the forms of idealism and skepticism that were prevalent in England at about the turn of the 20th century, the first major work of common sense philosophy was Moore's paper "A Defense of Common Sense" (1925). Against skepticism, Moore argued that he and other human beings have known many propositions about the world to be true with certainty. Among these propositions are: "The Earth has existed for many years" and "Many human beings have existed in the past and some still exist." Because skepticism maintains that nobody knows any proposition to be true, it can be dismissed. Furthermore, because these propositions entail the existence of material objects, idealism, according to which the world is wholly mental, can also be rejected. Moore called this outlook "the common sense view of the world," and he insisted that any philosophical system whose propositions contravene it can be rejected out of hand without further analysis.

ORDINARY LANGUAGE PHILOSOPHY

The two major proponents of ordinary language philosophy were the English philosophers Gilbert Ryle (1900–76) and J.L. Austin (1911–60). Although for different reasons, both held that philosophical problems frequently arise through a misuse or misunderstanding of ordinary speech. In *The Concept of Mind* (1949), Ryle argued that the traditional conception of the human mind—that it is an invisible, ghostlike entity occupying a physical body—is based on what he called a "category mistake." The mistake is to interpret the term *mind* as though it were analogous to the term *body* and thus to assume that both terms denote entities, one visible (body) and the other invisible (mind). His diagnosis of this error involved an elaborate description of how mental epithets actually work in ordinary speech. To speak of intelligence, for example, is to describe how human beings respond to certain kinds of problematic situations. Despite the behaviourist flavour of his analyses, Ryle insisted that he was not a behaviourist and that he was instead "charting the logical geography" of the mental concepts used in everyday life.

Austin's emphasis was somewhat different. In a celebrated paper, "A Plea for Excuses" (1956), he explained that the appeal to ordinary language in philosophy should be regarded as the first word but not the last word. That is, one should be sensitive to the nuances of everyday speech in approaching conceptual problems, but in certain circumstances everyday speech can, and should, be augmented by technical concepts. According to the "first-word" principle, because certain distinctions have been drawn in ordinary language for eons (e.g., males from females, friends from enemies, and so forth) one can conclude not only that the drawing of such distinctions is essential to everyday life but also that such distinctions are more than merely verbal. They pick out, or discriminate, actual features of the world. Starting from this principle, Austin dealt with major philosophical difficulties, such as the problem of other minds, the nature of truth, and the nature of responsibility.

SPEECH ACT THEORY

Austin was also the creator of one of the most original philosophical theories of the 20th century: speech act theory. A speech act is an utterance that is grammatically similar to a statement but is neither true nor false, though it is perfectly meaningful. For example, the utterance "I do," performed in the normal circumstances of marrying, is neither true nor false. It is not a statement but an action—a speech act—the primary effect of which is to complete the marriage ceremony. Similar considerations apply to utterances such as "I christen thee the *Joseph Stalin*," performed in the normal circumstances of christening a ship. Austin called such utterances "performatives" to indicate that, in making them, one is not only saying something but also doing something.

The theory of speech acts was, in effect, a profound criticism of the positivist thesis that every meaningful sentence is either true or false. The positivist view, according to Austin, embodies a "descriptive fallacy," in the sense that it treats the descriptive function of language as primary and more or less ignores other functions. Austin's account of speech acts was thus a corrective to that tendency.

After Austin's death in 1960, speech act theory was deepened and refined by his American student John R. Searle. In *The Construction of Social Reality* (1995), Searle argued that many social and political institutions are created through speech acts. Money, for example, is created through a declaration by a government to the effect that pieces of paper or metal of a certain manufacture and design are to count as money. Many institutions, such as banks, universities, and police departments, are social entities created through similar speech acts. Searle's development of speech act theory was thus an unexpected extension of the philosophy of language into social and political theory.

CONTINENTAL PHILOSOPHY

Until the late 20th century, analytic philosophy had comparatively little influence on the European continent, where the speculative and historical tradition remained strong. Dominated by phenomenology and existentialism during the first half of the 20th century, after World War II Continental philosophy came to embrace increasingly far-reaching structuralist and post-structuralist critiques of metaphysics and philosophical rationality.

THE PHENOMENOLOGY OF EDMUND HUSSERL AND MARTIN HEIDEGGER

Considered the father of phenomenology, Edmund Husserl (1859–1938), a German mathematician-turned-philosopher, was an extremely complicated and technical

Edmund Husserl, c. 1930. Archiv für Kunst und Geschichte, Berlin

thinker whose views changed considerably over the years. His chief contributions were the phenomenological method, which he developed early in his career, and the concept of the "life-world," which appeared only in his later writings. As a technique of phenomenological analysis, the phenomenological method was to make possible "a descriptive account of the essential structures of the directly given." It was to isolate and lay bare the intrinsic structure of conscious experience by focusing the philosopher's attention on the pure data of consciousness, uncontaminated by metaphysical theories or scientific or empirical assumptions of any kind. Husserl's concept of the life-world is similarly concerned with immediate experience. It is the individual's personal world as he directly experiences it, with the ego at the centre and with all of its vital and emotional colourings.

With the appearance of the *Jahrbuch für Philosophie und phänomenologische Forschung* (1913–30; "Annual for Philosophical and Phenomenological Research") under Husserl's chief editorship, his philosophy flowered into an international movement. Its most notable adherent was Martin Heidegger (1889–1976), whose masterpiece, *Sein und Zeit* (*Being and Time*), appeared in the *Jahrbuch* in 1927. The influence of the phenomenological method is clear in Heidegger's work; throughout his startlingly original investigations of human existence—with their unique dimensions of "being-in-the-world," dread, care, and "being-toward-death"—Heidegger adheres to the phenomenological principle that philosophy is not empirical but is the strictly self-evident insight into the structure of experience. Later, the French philosophical psychologist Maurice Merleau-Ponty (1908–61), building on the concept of the life-world, used the notions of the lived body and its "facticity" to create a hierarchy of human-lived experience.

THE EXISTENTIALISM OF KARL JASPERS AND JEAN-PAUL SARTRE

Existentialism, true to its roots in Kierkegaard and Nietzsche, was oriented toward two major themes: the analysis of human existence, or Being, and the centrality of human choice. Thus its chief theoretical energies were devoted to ontology and decision.

Existentialism as a philosophy of human existence was best expressed in the work of the German philosopher Karl Jaspers (1883–1969), who came to philosophy from medicine and psychology. For Jaspers as for Dewey, the aim of philosophy is practical. But whereas for Dewey philosophy is to guide human action, for Jaspers its purpose is the revelation of Being, "the illumination of existence," the answering of the questions of what human beings are and what they can become. This illumination is achieved, and Being is revealed most profoundly, through the experience of "extreme" situations that define the human condition—conflict, guilt, suffering, and death. It is through a confrontation with these extremes that the individual realizes his existential humanity.

The chief representative of existentialism as a philosophy of human decision was the French philosopher and man of letters Jean-Paul Sartre (1905–80). Sartre too was concerned with Being and with the dread experienced before the threat of Nothingness. But he found the essence of this Being in liberty: in freedom of choice and the duty of self-determination. He therefore devoted much effort to describing the human tendency toward "bad faith," reflected in perverse attempts to deny one's own responsibility and to flee from the truth of one's inescapable freedom. Sartre did not overlook the legitimate obstacles to freedom presented by the facts of place, past, environment, society, and death. However, he demanded

Jean-Paul Sartre, photograph by Gisèle Freund, 1968. Gisèle Freund

that one surmount these limitations through acts of conscious decision, for only in acts of freedom does human existence achieve authenticity. In *Le Deuxième Sexe*, 2 vol. (1949; *The Second Sex*), Simone de Beauvoir (1908–86), Sartre's fellow philosopher and lifelong companion, attempted to mobilize the existentialist concept of freedom for the ends of modern feminism.

After World War II Sartre came to believe that his philosophy of freedom had wrongly ignored problems of social justice. In his later work, especially the *Critique de la raison dialectique* (1960; *Critique of Dialectical Reason*), he sought to reconcile existentialism with Marxism.

CONTINENTAL PHILOSOPHY SINCE THE 1950S

The main theme of postwar Continental philosophy was the enthusiastic reception in France of Nietzsche and Heidegger and the consequent rejection of metaphysics and the Cartesian rationalism inherited by Sartre and his fellow existentialists. For millennia the goal of metaphysics, or "first philosophy," had been to discern the ultimate nature of reality. Postwar Continental philosophy, recoiling from omnipresent images of mass annihilation, increasingly held metaphysical holism itself responsible for the catastrophes of 20th-century history. The critics of metaphysics argued that only a relentless castigation of such excesses could produce a philosophy that was genuinely open toward Being, "thinghood," and world.

In the 1950s, French philosophy faced a series of major challenges arising from structuralism, the new movement in anthropology that analyzed cultures as systems of structurally related elements and attempted to discern universal patterns underlying all such systems. In his *Tristes tropiques* (1955; Eng. trans. *A World on the Wane*), for example, the anthropologist Claude Lévi-Strauss (1908–2009) issued a pointed indictment of philosophical method, claiming that it lacked empirical grounding and was so arbitrary as to be capable of proving or disproving anything. Sartre's political missteps during the early 1950s, when he had been an enthusiastic fellow traveler of the French Communist Party, did little to enhance the credibility of his philosophical rationalism.

In his influential book *Les Mots et les choses* (1966; Eng. trans. *The Order of Things*), Michel Foucault paradoxically employed structuralist methods to criticize the scientific pretensions of natural history, linguistics, and political economy, the disciplines known in France as the "human sciences." But the main target of his critique was the anthropocentric orientation of the humanities, notably including philosophy. Foucault argued provocatively that "man" was an artificial notion, an invention of the 19th century, and that its obsolescence had become apparent in the postwar era.

In later books such as *Surveiller et punir: naissance de la prison* (1975; *Discipline and Punish: The Birth of the Prison*) and *Histoire de la sexualité*, 3 vols. (1976–84; *The History of Sexuality*), Foucault's gaze shifted to systems of power. In a Nietzschean spirit, he coined the term *power-knowledge* to indicate the involvement of knowledge in the maintenance of power relations. As he argued in the essay "Nietzsche, Genealogy, History" (1977), an examination of the notion of truth reveals that

all knowledge rests upon injustice, that there is no right, not even in the act of knowing, to truth or a foundation for truth, and that the instinct for knowledge is malicious (something murderous, opposed to the happiness of mankind).

The movement known as deconstruction, derived mainly from work begun in the 1960s by Jacques Derrida, displayed a similar hostility to metaphysics and its quest for totality and absolute truth. Under the sway of Heidegger's call for "a destruction of the history of ontology," Derrida endorsed the deconstruction of Western philosophy (i.e., the uncovering and undoing of the false dichotomies, or "oppositions," inherent in philosophical thinking since the time of the ancient Greeks). In Derrida's view, these oppositions result from the misguided assumption, which he called "logocentrism," that there is a realm of truth that exists prior to and independently of its representation by linguistic and other signs. Logocentrism in turn derives from the "metaphysics of presence," or the tendency to conceive of fundamental philosophical concepts such as truth, reality, and being in terms of ideas such as identity, presence, and essence and to limit or ignore the equally valid notions of otherness, absence, and difference. Because of this tendency, Derrida concluded, there is a necessary relationship between the metaphysical quest for "totality" and political "totalitarianism." As he wrote in an early essay, "Violence and Metaphysics" (1967):

> *Incapable of respecting the Being and meaning of the other, phenomenology and ontology would be philosophies of violence. Through them, the entire philosophical tradition... would make common cause with oppression and technico-political possession.*

The French philosopher Emmanuel Lévinas (1905–95) attributed the misguided quest for totality to a defect in reason itself. In his major work, *Totalité et infini* (1961; *Totality and Infinity*), he contended that, as it is used in Western philosophy, reason enforces "domination" and "sameness" and destroys plurality and otherness. He called for the transcendence of reason in a first philosophy based

on ethics—and in particular on the biblical command-
ment "You shall not kill" (Exodus 20:13)—rather than on
logic. It is no small irony, then, that Continental philosophy, whose roots lay in the attempt by Kant, Hegel, and
their successors to defend reason against the twin excesses
of dogmatism and epistemological skepticism, should
come to equate reason with domination and to insist that
reason's hegemony be overthrown.

A powerful alternative to this view appeared in
work from the 1970s by the German philosopher
Jürgen Habermas. Although agreeing with the French
Nietzscheans that traditional metaphysics was obsolete
and, in particular, that it did not provide a path to absolute truth, Habermas did not reject the notion of truth
entirely, nor did he accept the Nietzscheans' call for a
"farewell to reason." While acknowledging that the notion
of truth is often used to mask unjust power relations and
partisan class interests, he insisted that the very possibility of such an insight presupposes that one can conceive of
social relations that are just and interests that are held in
common by all members of society.

Habermas's *Theorie des kommunikativen Handelns*, 2
vols. (1981; *Theory of Communicative Action*) was devoted in
part to developing an account of truth in terms that did
not imply that there exists an "absolute" truth of the kind
traditionally posited by metaphysics. Following the doctrines of pragmatism and reinterpreting Austin's earlier
work on speech acts, Habermas contended that ordinary
communication differs from other forms of human action
in that it is oriented toward mutual agreement rather than
"success." That is, it aims at reaching "intersubjective"
understanding rather than at mastering the world through
instrumental action. The process of constructing such an
understanding, however, requires that each individual
assume that the utterances of the other are for the most

part "true" and that the other can provide reasons to support the truth or validity of his utterance if called upon to do so. Specifically, individuals must interpret each other's utterances as true assertions about objects and events in an "external world," as descriptions of morally "right" actions in a social world of shared norms, or as "sincere" expressions of thoughts and feelings in the speaker's "inner world." In this "discourse theory of truth," the notion of truth, far from being a misguided fiction of metaphysics, is a regulative ideal without which communication itself would be impossible.

THE RELEVANCE OF CONTEMPORARY PHILOSOPHY

Despite the tradition of philosophical professionalism established during the Enlightenment, philosophy in the 19th century was still created largely outside the universities. Comte, Mill, Marx, Schopenhauer, and Kierkegaard were not professors, and only the German idealist school was rooted in academic life. Since the early 20th century, however, most well-known philosophers have been associated with academia. It is perhaps not surprising, therefore, that philosophers in both the analytic and the Continental traditions have come to employ a technical vocabulary and to deal with narrow, specialized, or esoteric problems and that their strictly philosophical work has been addressed not to a broad intellectual public but to one another. Professionalism also has sharpened the divisions between philosophical schools and made the question of what philosophy is and what it ought to be a matter of the sharpest controversy. Philosophy has become extremely self-conscious about its own methods and nature.

These trends, among others, have seemed to lend support to intellectual critics of contemporary philosophy who argue that it has lost sight of its purpose—that it fails to address deep human problems and concerns, that it does little if anything to make the universe or human life more intelligible or meaningful. These complaints are distinct from (but obviously related to) the age-old accusation that philosophy is of no "practical" benefit or import (a charge that is easily refuted, as there would have been no Declaration of Independence without Locke). Although it is true that specialization—a concentration on "small" questions—has become a common phenomenon within philosophy since the early 20th century, as it has in nearly all other academic disciplines, it would be a gross exaggeration to say that philosophy is no longer concerned with the "big" questions traditionally associated with it—questions about the ultimate nature of reality; the scope and limits of human knowledge; the nature of moral right and wrong, good and bad; the extent of people's moral rights, duties, and obligations; the relation of the mind to the body (or the mental to the material); and so on. These problems continue to be addressed by both analytic and Continental philosophers, albeit sometimes in language that is difficult for non-philosophers to understand. Philosophy continues to offer enriching insight into these deep issues, and for that reason it remains— as it always was—a fundamentally important human endeavour.

anarchism Doctrines and attitudes rooted in the belief that government is harmful as well as unnecessary.

atomism Any theory that attempts to explain changes of gross physical bodies in terms of the motions of minute indivisible particles.

Averroists A group of masters in the faculty of arts at Paris who based their interpretations of Aristotle's philosophy on the commentaries of the Arabic philosopher Averroës.

axiom A principle or maxim accepted without proof that serves as a basis for further analysis.

Cartesianism Philosophical and scientific traditions based on the writings Descartes.

Deism Religious attitude that accepted the following: principles the existence of one God, often conceived of as architect or mechanician, the existence of a system of rewards and punishments administered by that God, and the obligation to be virtuous and pious.

empirical claim Claim that is about something that can in principle be experienced.

fortuna Play of external forces.

humanism System of education and mode of inquiry that emphasized human concerns.

perspectivism The view that all knowledge is situated and partial.

Platonism Any philosophy that derives its ultimate inspiration from Plato.

primary qualities Properties of a thing that resemble the ideas they cause in the mind (size, shape, weight, and solidity).

Pyrrhic Accomplished at exorbitant sacrifice, often cancelling out or overriding anticipated benefits.

satire Artistic form that holds up vices, follies, abuses, or shortcomings to censure with ridicule, derision, burlesque, irony, parody, caricature, or other methods.

Scholasticism Philosophical systems and speculative tendencies of various medieval Christian thinkers from the 11th through the 14th century.

secondary qualities Properties of a thing that cause sensible ideas but do not resemble them.

skepticism The doctrine or practice of systematic doubt of knowledge claims set forth in various areas.

social dynamics Study of the causes of social change.

social responsibility Any general moral obligation to others or to society as a whole.

social statics Study of the forces that hold society together.

solipsism In epistemology, the view that the mind or subject has no good reason to believe in the existence of anything other than itself.

Stoicism Belief that the goal of all inquiry is to provide a mode of conduct characterized by tranquility of mind and certainty of moral worth.

syncretism In philosophy and religion, doctrine that stresses the unity and compatibility of different schools and systems.

tautology Statement that it cannot be denied without inconsistency.

universal Quality or property that each individual member of a class of things must possess if the same general word is to apply to all the things in that class.

utilitarianism In ethics, doctrine that actions should be judged by the extent to which they promote the greatest happiness of the greatest number.

utopian An ideal or perfect society.

virtù Bold and intelligent initiative.

RENAISSANCE PHILOSOPHY

Ernst Cassirer, *The Individual and the Cosmos in Renaissance Philosophy*, trans. by Mario Domandi (1963, reissued 2000; originally published in German, 1927), is an important study. Ernst Cassirer, John H. Randall, and Paul O. Kristeller (eds.), *Renaissance Philosophy of Man* (1948, reprinted 1993), is a collection of important Renaissance philosophical statements translated into English, some for the first time. The author of the following works, Paul O. Kristeller, was one of the leading 20th-century scholars of the Renaissance: *The Classics and Renaissance Thought*, rev. ed. (1961, reissued 1969); *Eight Philosophers of the Italian Renaissance* (1964, reprinted 1966); *Medieval Aspects of Renaissance Learning*, ed. and trans. by Edward P. Mahoney (1974, reissued 1992); and *Renaissance Concepts of Man, and Other Essays*, ed. by Michael Mooney (1972, reissued 1979). Brian P. Copenhaver and Charles B. Schmitt, *Renaissance Philosophy* (1992, reissued 1997), a fine exposition of many aspects of Renaissance philosophy, was drafted by Schmitt and finished after his death by Copenhaver. Charles B. Schmitt et al. (eds.), *Cambridge History of Renaissance Philosophy* (1988), is a collection of essays by leading scholars.

EARLY MODERN AND CONTEMPORARY PHILOSOPHY

Noteworthy studies include Kuno Fischer, *History of Modern Philosophy: Descartes and His School*, ed. by Noah Porter and trans. by J.P. Goody (1887, reissued 1992; originally published as vol. 1 of his *Geschichte der neuern Philosophie*, 11 vol., 1878); Richard H. Popkin (ed.), *The*

Philosophy of the Sixteenth and Seventeenth Centuries (1966); Tom Sorell (ed.), *The Rise of Modern Philosophy: The Tension Between the New and Traditional Philosophies from Machiavelli to Leibniz* (1993), a collection of essays by various scholars; Ernst Cassirer, *The Philosophy of the Enlightenment*, trans. by J. Pettigrove and F. Koelin (1951, reissued 1979; originally published in German, 1932); Johann Eduard Erdmann, *A History of Philosophy*, trans. by Williston S. Hough, 3 vol. (1890, reissued 1997; originally published in German, 2 vol., 1878); and Harald Høffding, *A History of Modern Philosophy*, trans. by B.E. Meyer, 2 vol. (1900, reissued 1958; trans. from the 1895–96 German ed.; originally published in Danish, 1894–95).

More contemporary works include Raymond Klibansky (ed.), *Philosophy in the Mid-Century: A Survey*, 3rd ed., 4 vol. (1967), and *Contemporary Philosophy: A Survey*, 4 vol. (1968, reissued 1971), a collection of essays by leading scholars; Albert William Levi, *Philosophy and the Modern World* (1959, reissued 1977), a broad treatment, and *Philosophy as Social Expression* (1974); Wolfgang Stegmüller, *Main Currents in Contemporary German, British, and American Philosophy*, trans. by Albert L. Blumberg (1970; originally published in German, 4th ed., 1969), a narrower, more technical treatment; Walter Kaufmann (ed.), *Existentialism from Dostoevsky to Sartre*, rev. and expanded ed. (1975, reissued 2004), selections with introductions; and Marvin Farber (ed.), *Philosophic Thought in France and the United States: Essays Representing Major Trends in Contemporary French and American Philosophy*, 2nd ed. (1968; originally published in French, 1950).

INDEX

A

Adorno, Theodor, 183
  Dialectic of Enlightenment, 185
Alberti, Leon Battista, 30, 31, 33
analytic philosophy, 176
  formalist tradition, 195–200
  informalist tradition, 195,
    200–203
  overview of, 194–195
Aquinas, Saint Thomas, 21, 45,
    91, 104, 115
Arendt, Hannah, 187–189
  Eichmann in Jerusalem, 187–189
  The Human Condition, 187
  Origins of Totalitarianism, 187
Aristotle, 22, 34, 44, 49, 53, 54,
    63, 65, 68, 70, 71, 78, 79, 81,
    92, 126, 172, 182
Arnauld, Antoine, 95, 97
astronomy, 54, 67–68, 70, 79,
    104, 155
Augustine, Saint, 35, 45, 61, 91,
    111, 115, 168
Austin, J.L., 201–203, 211
  "A Plea for Excuses," 201–202
Averroës, Ibn-Rushd, 68, 71

B

Bacon, Sir Francis, 21, 30, 51,
    75–82, 84, 92, 93, 97, 104,
    108, 153
  Advancement of Learning, 76, 79
  idols of the mind, 79–81
  inductive reasoning, 81–82, 160

Novum Organum, 76, 78, 79,
    81–82
Beauvoir, Simone de, 208
  The Second Sex, 208
Bentham, Jeremy, 107, 124,
    157–158
  *Introduction to the Principles of
    Morals and Legislation*, 157
Bergson, Henri, 174–175
Berkeley, George, 109, 112–115
  *Treatise Concerning the Principles
    of Human Knowledge*, 113
Boccaccio, Giovanni, 30, 31
Bodin, Jean, 47, 48, 66–67, 125
Bradley, F.H., 144, 164
Bruni, Leonardo, 37–38
Bruno, Giordano, 32, 45, 67–74
  dialogues, 70–71

C

Cartesian Circle, 97
Castiglione, Baldassare, 30, 33–34
Christianity, 19, 35–36, 38, 39,
    42–44, 53, 65, 68–69, 71,
    74, 103–104, 115, 137, 138,
    154, 156
Cicero, 27, 65
common sense philosophy,
    200–201
communism, 163, 178, 182, 209
communitarianism, 194
Comte, Auguste, 144, 153–156,
    160, 212
  *The Positive Philosophy of
    Auguste Comte*, 153